Social Skills Training
Treatment for Depression

*- Feeling good: The new
mood therapy*

- David Burns MD

Pergamon Titles of Related Interest

Cartledge / Milburn TEACHING SOCIAL SKILLS TO CHILDREN:
Innovative Approaches, Second Edition
Goldstein / PSYCHOLOGICAL SKILL TRAINING:
The Structured Learning Technique
Gotlib / Colby TREATMENT OF DEPRESSION:
An Interpersonal Systems Approach
Hollin / Trower HANDBOOK OF SOCIAL SKILLS TRAINING,
Vols. 1 & 2
Liberman / Mueser SOCIAL SKILLS TRAINING FOR
PSYCHIATRIC PATIENTS
Yost / Beutler / Corbishley / Allender
GROUP COGNITIVE THERAPY:
A Treatment Approach for Depressed Older Adults

Related Journals *

CLINICAL PSYCHOLOGY REVIEW
* Free sample copies available upon request

PSYCHOLOGY PRACTITIONER GUIDEBOOKS

EDITORS

Arnold P. Goldstein, Syracuse University
Leonard Krasner, Stanford University & SUNY at Stony Brook
Sol L. Garfield, Washington University

Social Skills Training Treatment for Depression

ROBERT E. BECKER
Medical College of Pennsylvania at
Eastern Pennsylvania Psychiatric Institute

RICHARD G. HEIMBERG
State University of New York at Albany

ALAN S. BELLACK
Medical College of Pennsylvania at
Eastern Pennsylvania Psychiatric Institute

PERGAMON PRESS

New York · Oxford · Beijing · Frankfurt
São Paulo · Sydney · Tokyo · Toronto

U.S.A.	Pergamon Press, Maxwell House, Fairview Park, Elmsford, New York 10523, U.S.A.
U.K.	Pergamon Press, Headington Hill Hall, Oxford OX3 0BW, England
PEOPLE'S REPUBLIC OF CHINA	Pergamon Press, Room 4037, Qianmen Hotel, Beijing, People's Republic of China
FEDERAL REPUBLIC OF GERMANY	Pergamon Press, Hammerweg 6, D-6242 Kronberg, Federal Republic of Germany
BRAZIL	Pergamon Editora, Rua Eca de Queiros, 346, CEP 04011, Paraiso, São Paulo, Brazil
AUSTRALIA	Pergamon Press Australia, P.O. Box 544, Potts Point, N.S.W. 2011, Australia
JAPAN	Pergamon Press, 8th Floor, Matsuoka Central Building, 1-7-1 Nishishinjuku, Shinjuku-ku, Tokyo 160, Japan
CANADA	Pergamon Press Canada, Suite No. 271, 253 College Street, Toronto, Ontario, Canada M5T 1R5

First edition 1987

Library of Congress Cataloging in Publication Data

Becker, Robert E.
Social skills training treatment for depression.
(Psychology practitioner guidebooks)
Bibliography: p.
Includes indexes.
1. Depression, Mental — Treatment. 2. Social skills — Therapeutic use. I. Heimberg, Richard G. II. Bellack, Alan S. III. Title. IV. Series. [DNLM: 1. Behavior Therapy. 2. Depression — therapy. WM 171 B396s]
RC537.B434 1987 616.85'2706 87–10424

British Library Cataloguing in Publication Data

Becker, Robert E.
Social skills training treatment for depression.
— (Psychology practitioner guidebooks)
1. Depression, Mental — Treatment
2. Behavior therapy
I. Title II. Heimberg, Richard G.
III. Bellack, Alan S. IV Series
616.85'2706 RC537

ISBN 0-08-032818-0 Hardcover
ISBN 0-08-032817-2 Flexicover

Printed in Great Britain by
Hazell Watson & Viney Limited,
Member of the BPCC Group,
Aylesbury, Bucks

Table of Contents

Preface

This volume represents the culmination of our thinking about *social skills training* as a treatment for depressed outpatients. Many years of clinical experience, careful thought, and trial and error have gone before. Our purpose in this volume is to advance the field of psychological treatment for depression by providing practitioners with a clear, descriptive manual. Our effort in this regard has spurred us to include descriptive case material, numerous tables, and concise summaries of our clinical strategies.

This volume is intended for use by practicing clinicians and by graduate students learning to carry out psychotherapy treatments. It is not intended to be a self-help manual. Clinicians who are already familiar with a behavioral conceptualization of psychopathology will find the book easier to understand.

A number of historical events have contributed to this book. These ideas germinated in 1978 and 1979 as Drs. Becker and Heimberg first began to work together. It was during this time that we became aware of the pioneering work of our colleagues Drs. Alan Bellack and Michel Hersen. Much of their work and thinking is reflected in this volume.

Under the direction of Robert F. Prien, PhD, the National Institute of Mental Health (NIMH) was carrying out a collaborative study aimed at the treatment of depression. This study afforded an opportunity to learn an enormous amount about depression. The assistance given by Dr. Prien was of great value to us. As a result, Drs. Becker and Heimberg proposed another study to the NIMH. This study allowed social skills ideas to flourish and also provided the opportunity to get to know, and later work with, Dr. Bellack.

Many other people have assisted us in our endeavours. Special thanks include those to David Gansler; Ann Mundt; Emil Chiauzzi, PhD; Rod McIntosh RPA; Sandy Agosto; Barbara Gillen, MA; Ruth Morelli, PhD; Kasinath Yadalam, MD; Eileen Michaels, MA; Ralph Carotenuto, MD; Ed Sorenson, MD; Peter Mansky, MD; Margery Brown, PhD; Ed Blanchard, PhD, and Chris Blanchard, PhD. A particular thanks goes to Reuben Silver, PhD for his unswerving support and encouragement.

Of course we cannot neglect our families, for they gave the most in understanding when we were busy and encouragement when we felt frustrated.
Robert E. Becker
Richard G. Heimberg
Alan S. Bellack

Chapter 1
Introduction

Recent data from epidemiological studies demonstrate that depressive disorders are among the most serious public-health concerns. For example, consider the lifetime risk of a depressive disorder. *Lifetime prevalence* is the percentage of a birth cohort that will experience a particular disorder at some point during their lives. Data from recent National Institute of Mental Health studies suggest a lifetime prevalence of affective disorder from a low of 6.1% to a high of 9.5%. Major depressive disorder makes up the largest segment of this group, with a range of 3.7% to 6.7% of the population, followed by dysthymic disorder, with a range of 2.1% to 3.8%. Trailing farther behind is manic disorder, with 0.6% to 1.1% of the population (Robins et al., 1984).

These data imply that a large segment of the United States population will experience an affective episode in their lifetimes. The toll in human suffering, lost opportunity, dashed hopes, and loss of life to suicide is truly significant. Examination of shorter intervals of time indicates that large numbers of people experience an affective disturbance at any given time. For example, *6-month point prevalence* is the percentage of the population suffering from an affective disorder during any specified 6-month interval. Six-month point prevalence figures are expectedly lower than lifetime prevalence, yet they are still substantial, with major depressive disorder having a 2.2%–3.5% rate, dysthymic disorder having a 2.1%–3.2% rate, and mania having a 0.4%–0.8% rate (Meyers et al., 1984). Applying these rates to the approximate United States population of 250 million implies that 8 million persons will suffer from major depressive disorder, 7 million from dysthymic disorder, and 2 million from mania during any 6-month interval.

Evidence from epidemiological studies implicates a number of variables related to depression. Foremost among these is gender. This variable has been the most extensively studied and has shown the most consistent results. Women experience higher rates of depressive symptoms than men (Brown & Harris, 1978; Robins et al., 1984). More recent data suggest that sex cannot be considered alone. Ensel (1982) noted that sex differences in depression vary

1

with age a.1d marital status. He found that unmarried females were the most depressed of all sex-by-marital-status groupings. Among married persons, young married females were most likely to be depressed. When young married women were excluded, there was no difference in depression between married men and married women.

Marital status, separately from age and sex, has been associated with higher rates of depressive disorders. Comstock and Helsing (1976) and Weissman and Meyers (1978) have both reported higher rates of depressive symptoms in divorced and separated persons than in married persons. Age also has been implicated as being related to depressive disorder.

Depressive disorder appears to be significantly more prevalent among younger adults and less prevalent among the elderly (Weissman et al., 1984). Six-month point prevalence data suggest that depressive disorders are most prevalent in individuals under 45 years of age. The prevalence of major depressive disorders appears to decline with increasing age. Other studies (Dean & Ensel, 1982, 1983a, 1983b; Schwab, Bell, Warheit, & Schwab, 1979) have also reported a similar decline in the prevalence of depressive disorder with increasing age.

Depressive disorders affect a large number of individuals and constitute a significant portion of complaints from clients. In a similar vein, treatment of these disorders is an important undertaking for many practitioners and clinics. Many agencies have chosen to run specialty clinics focused exclusively on the diagnosis and treatment of depressive disorders. A variety of pharmacotherapeutic and psychotherapeutic approaches are currently available. Our purpose is to share with you the psychotherapeutic technique called *social skills training.* This technique is a combination of procedures that attempt to teach clients to achieve meaningful interpersonal relationships, to accurately and clearly communicate with others, and to accurately evaluate themselves and reward their own behaviour adaptively. Treatment includes direct training of interpersonal behavior via instruction, demonstration, role play, coaching, and practice. Adaptive self-evaluation and self-reinforcement is another critical component.

This is a comprehensive treatment that directly addresses the problems and concerns of many depressed patients. It has been shown to be effective in the treatment of clients with major depressive disorder (Hersen, Bellack, Himmelhoch, & Thase, 1984) and dysthymic disorder (Becker & Heimberg, 1985).

In this volume we hope to provide the practicing clinician with enough information about the techniques of *social skills training* that he or she will feel reasonably competent to apply these techniques to depressed patients. Without a basis in theory, many clinicians fail to see the rationale for the application of social skills training. To assist these clinicians, and our readers generally, in the whys and wherefores of this approach, we will conduct a selected review of the literature on the behavioral and cognitive styles of depressed persons. We will deliberately not conduct an exhaustive or critical review of this literature, for our purpose is not to point to anomalies in the assumptions or the data but to convey to our readers the current assumptions underlying social skills training. With this accomplished, we will turn our attention to more clinical matters and focus on two important tasks that should be carried out prior to the clinical application of any of these techniques, namely, the proper diagnosis of depression and the assessment of social skills. Subsequent to this necessary digression, we will turn our attention entirely to the clinical procedures employed in our version of social skills training. We have segregated this clinical discussion into five distinct chapters: (a) clinical assessment of social performance, (b) direct behavior training, (c) practice and generalization, (d) social perception training, and (e) self-evaluation and self-reinforcement training. We wish to caution the reader that, although the presentation of each set of techniques is segregated, the application of the entire package is done in an *integrated fashion*. It is easier to describe the procedures separately, but the application is much more effective and efficient when conducted in an intermingled fashion. We then follow these sections with a discussion of specific problems the clinician could encounter while conducting social skills training, along with some suggested solutions to these problems. Each section contains liberal doses of case examples including common mistakes or misapplications of techniques.

The first task is to review selected, relevant studies that highlight the underpinnings of a social skills training approach to treatment. We now turn to this task.

Chapter 2
Background Literature

In this chapter we will describe the theoretical and empirical bases for the techniques employed in social skills training and review the support for its effectiveness. As we noted earlier, this treatment package consists of a number of discrete components administered in an integrated fashion. These include: (a) clinical assessment of social performance, (b) direct behavior training, (c) practice and generalization, (d) socialperception training, (e) self-evaluation and self-reinforcement training.

We have developed the social skills training program on the premise that depressive behavior is related to inadequate interpersonal functioning. Becker and Heimberg (1985, pp. 205–206) described several corollary assumptions that guided these efforts:

1. Depression is a result of an inadequate schedule of positive reinforcement contingent on the person's nondepressed behavior.
2. A meaningful portion of the most salient positive reinforcers in the adult world are interpersonal in nature.
3. A meaningful portion of the non-interpersonal rewards in adult life may be received or denied, contingent on the person's interpersonal behavior.
4. Therefore, any set of treatment techniques that helps the depressed patient increase the quality of his or her interpersonal behavior should act to increase the amount of response-contingent positive reinforcement and thereby decrease depressive affect and increase the rate of "nondepressed behavior."
5. Inadequate interpersonal behavior may arise from any number of sources including, but not restricted to, the following:
   a. Insufficient exposure to interpersonally skilled models at key developmental periods.
   b. Insufficient opportunity to practice important interpersonal routines at key developmental periods.

c. Learning of inappropriate or maladaptive interpersonal behaviors at key developmental periods.

d. Failure to "discard" old behaviors and adopt new ones during periods of transition, that is, entry into adolescence or adulthood.

e. Decaying of specific behavioral skills due to disuse, as in the case of a newly divorced individual who must now enter the singles' world.

f. Failure to recognize the appropriate or inappropriate times for the execution of specific behavioral routines.

g. Failure to execute adaptive behavior because of a belief that it will not produce the desired results or one's belief that he or she cannot perform the required behavior adequately.

These statements are based on a large body of literature about the behavioral analysis of depression, the interpersonal behavior of depressed and nondepressed persons, and the cognitive processes of depressed and nondepressed persons. All the statements under point 5 also represent the justification for the specific techniques of social skills training: direct behavior training (5a–5e), social perception training (5f), and self-evaluation and self-reinforcement training (5g). We now examine the relationship between depression and both positive reinforcement and interpersonal behavior.

DEPRESSION AND POSITIVE REINFORCEMENT

Charles Ferster (1965, 1973), the first behavioral psychologist to devote his attention to the study of depression, defined depression as a low rate of operant behavior emitted by an individual. The low rate of behavior was said to result from a disruption in the person's ongoing system of positive reinforcement. In behavioral terms, the person's behavior is placed on extinction, that is, it is no longer being reinforced. Without reinforcement, the behavior occurs at a lower rate, setting in motion a vicious cycle that further reduces opportunities for reinforcement: less reinforcement leads to less behavior, leads to less opportunity for reinforcement, leads to less reinforcement, leads to less behavior, and on and on. If the amount of positive reinforcement a person receives should drop low enough, then depression should result.

A reduction in the amount of available reinforcement might occur for any number of reasons including death of a spouse or loved one, loss of a job, crippling or life-threatening illness or injury, divorce, and anxiety inhibiting a person's freedom of movement (such as the side effects that result from severe agoraphobia or social phobia). These events reduce the amount of response-contingent positive reinforcement available to the person by removing the source of reward from the environment (such as through divorce) or by denying her or him access to available rewards. That reduction leads to the extinction of behaviors that were previously maintained by those rewards, and the resultant lowered rate of behavior provides even fewer reinforcement opportunities. The person becomes increasingly passive and emits fewer behaviors that are "reinforceable." Depressive affect ensues.

An example might clarify Ferster's ideas. Let's consider the case of a 40-year-old man who became divorced after 19 years of marriage. For years he had worked very long and hard at an unsatisfying job. He had derived most of his pleasure in life from time spent with his wife and children, a daughter, 16, and a son, 18. In the last few years, as the children had grown older and more independent, he and his wife had spent increasing amounts of time together. For reasons that we need not go into here, the marriage rapidly deteriorated into divorce. The man became depressed and remained so even after many months had passed. He spent most of his off-work hours sitting at home, doing little other than recalling days gone by and how much he had lost. His job performance deteriorated, and he eventually quit going to work.

Ferster might suggest that the man's depression resulted from the fact that his wife had been his major source of positive reinforcement. Almost all of his activities beyond work had been shared with her. The excitement (reinforcing value) of many activities was extremely diminished when they were no longer shared. These activities were curtailed, and the amount of positive reinforcement experienced by the man was reduced. As his children grew older, he received less immediate and frequent positive reinforcement from them, thus exacerbating the problem. He found himself going out of his house less and less often, and, as a result, he sacrificed reinforcements from such varied sources as his daily chat with the local butcher and the enjoyment he received from reading the daily sporting news that he picked up every morning at the corner newsstand. He no longer went to work, so he no longer had everyday conversations around the coffee pot. Positive reinforcement of his behavior became an increasingly unlikely event, and he simply behaved less.

Ferster's formulations initiated the behavioral study of depression. However, they are not adequate to explain individual differences in the ways in which people respond to unpleasant life events. According to Ferster's model, any disruption of positive reinforcement systems should lead to depression, and anyone who experiences an unpleasant event should become depressed. However, this is clearly not the case. The association between depression and stressful life events is complex and poorly understood (Hammen, Mayol, deMayo, & Marks, 1986). Not everyone reacts to these events with depressive affect.

DEPRESSION AND
INTERPERSONAL BEHAVIOR

Peter Lewinsohn extended Ferster's theories to emphasize the role of interpersonal processes (Lewinsohn, 1975; Lewinsohn, Youngren, & Grosscup, 1979). Like Ferster, he emphasized the role of *response-contingent positive reinforcement.* It is not the total amount of good things in a person's life that is critical but rather the number and quality of good things that happen to someone as a result of his or her own behavior. The amount of response-contingent positive reinforcement is said to be a function of: (a) the number of activities the person might find potentially rewarding, (b) the availability of those events in the person's immediate environment, and (c) *the skillfulness and rate of emission of interpersonal behaviors that elicit a maximum of positive reinforcement and a minimum of punishment for the individual,* that is, social skill. According to Lewinsohn (1975), depression-prone persons are lacking in this important area. As a result, when they find their lives disrupted for any number of reasons, they might be less able than other persons to develop alternative sources of personal gratification.

According to this formulation, a person whose social-interactional repertoire is strong could show a mildly negative reaction to a powerful personal disruption, whereas a socially unskilled individual might react with depression to much lesser catastrophes. In the example of the divorced man who became depressed, Lewinsohn might hypothesize that his depression was related to lack of social skill. After a period of recovery from the shock of divorce, a socially skilled individual might have been able to meet people, develop new friendships, and form the basis of future intimate relationships. Newly formed friendships and relationships would supply a portion of the man's desired positive reinforcement. However, he lacked the social skills to do this; possibly these skills had fallen into disuse with his years of marriage. Being unable to do this, our gentleman was faced with a crisis of reinforcement, and depression resulted.

Several studies demonstrate the poor quality of the interpersonal behavior of depressed individuals. Although these studies do not indicate the specific reasons for deficits in social behavior, they provide support for many of Lewinsohn's contentions and suggest the importance of helping depressed individuals improve the level of their social performance. Coyne (1976a, 1976b) conducted the first study on the interpersonal interactions of depressed persons. He simply asked nondepressed subjects to spend time conversing with depressed individuals. Afterward, these nondepressed subjects reported a precipitous drop in their own moods. They also rated the conversations as decidedly unpleasant and expressed a desire to avoid the depressed persons in the future. The potential impact of this finding is striking. Depressed individuals might not only have difficulty developing new relationships but also actually drive people away from them. Although the significance of these findings continues to be debated (Coyne, 1985; Doerfler & Chaplin, 1985; Gurtman, 1986; King & Heller, 1984), similar findings have been reported by several investigators (Boswell & Murray, 1981; Hammen & Peters, 1978; Howes & Hokanson, 1979; Strack & Coyne, 1983).

A study by Jacobson and Anderson (1982) could shed some light on this reaction. Depressed and nondepressed subjects were paired for dyadic interactions. Conversations were recorded, and the frequencies of several categories were calculated. Whereas depressed and nondepressed subjects showed similar frequencies of most behaviors, depressed subjects made more negative self-referent statements. They also emitted more self-disclosing statements, presumably of the same negative tone, without being asked about these topics by their conversational partners. Additional research by Kuiper and McCabe (1985) suggests that depressed persons view negative conversational topics as more socially appropriate than nondepressed persons. It might be this tendency to talk about unsolicited negative topics that made Coyne's nondepressed subjects so uncomfortable.

Lewinsohn and his colleagues have repeatedly demonstrated that depressed individuals perform less adequately than nondepressed persons in group interactions. In several studies, observers rated depressed persons as less socially skilled (e.g., Lewinsohn, Mischel, Chaplin, & Barton, 1980). In a study by Libet and Lewinsohn (1973), depressed college students showed several deficits in social performance, including slower response time, less frequent initiation of conversation, and lower probability of rewarding the conversational initiations of others.

Another study, by Youngren and Lewinsohn (1980), demonstrated similar patterns among clinically depressed outpatients. Compared with normals and nondepressed psychiatric controls, depressed patients reported less frequent involvement in social activities and less reward from participating in such interactions. They also reported greater discomfort in social activities, in giving and receiving positive responses, and in behaving assertively. Difficulties in assertive behavior among depressed persons have been frequently reported (e.g., Langone, 1979; Lea & Pacquin, 1979). In a related study, Sanchez and Lewinsohn (1980) asked depressed outpatients to self-monitor their levels of depression and the rates with which they behaved assertively every day for a 5-week period. Assertive behavior and mood were negatively correlated. Moreover, assertive behavior was found to predict the next day's mood, whereas mood did not predict the next day's assertive behavior.

Clearly, depressed persons' social behavior can contribute to their depressed state in a number of ways. They initiate fewer social interactions, and those social interactions can prove punishing to the other persons involved, thus endangering future sources of social reinforcement. They tend to feel better if they stand up for themselves, but they tend not to do this. Although this description might not apply to all depressed persons, it appears important to carefully assess the social behavior of depressed patients and help them improve the quality of this behavior if necessary. This is the purpose of the portion of social skills training we call *direct behavior training*.

DEPRESSION, SOCIAL SKILL, AND SOCIAL PERCEPTION

Direct behavior training emphasizes the training of expressive communication skills. Clients are taught the components of assertive behavior and the skills necessary to initiate and maintain conversations with others. We might say that direct behavior training focuses on the *hows* of effective social behavior. The module labeled *social perception training* emphasizes the *wheres* and *whens* of effective social behavior. Morrison and Bellack (1981) reviewed several studies that implicated the ability to adequately receive and process interpersonal stimuli as essential for effective social performance. To perform skillfully, the individual must be able to identify the emotions or intent expressed by the other person and make sophisticated judgments about the form and timing of the appropriate response. Inaccurate conclusions about another person's intended meanings can be reached in a social interaction because a person fails to listen or look at the interaction partner, fails to integrate what is heard, does not know the meaning of what is heard, or looks for cues that are irrelevant to the moment. Such factors have been related to the inability of distressed marital partners to identify emotions expressed by their spouses and of unassertive psychiatric patients to select adaptive assertive responses (Morrison & Bellack, 1981). Although social perception has not been specifically linked to depression, we believe that the behaviors learned during direct behavior training cannot be adequately utilized without attention to these processes. We have used modules designed to train social perception skills in our social skills training packages (Becker & Heimberg, 1985; Bellack, Hersen, & Himmelhoch, 1980). Their application to the treatment of depressed patients will be detailed in later chapters.

DEPRESSION AND SELF-CONTROL

Rehm (1977) described depression as the result of a series of deficits in self-control processes. His model, derived from the work of Kanfer (1970, 1971) on behavioral self-control, addresses additional aspects of depression. We have borrowed several aspects of Rehm's model and incorporated these into our own treatment procedures.

According to Kanfer's formulations, self-control is the sum of those processes by which a person alters the probability of a response in the (more or less complete) absence of external supports. Three interrelated processes are implicated in behavioral self-control: self-monitoring, self-evaluation, and self-reinforcement.

Self-monitoring

Self-monitoring involves the observation of one's own behavior, along with its situational antecedents and reinforcing or punishing consequences. According to Rehm (1977), self-monitoring involves not only the passive awareness of events but also selective attention to certain classes of events. He asserted that depressed individuals demonstrate a tendency to selectively attend to negative events while overlooking positive outcomes. In fact, Wener and Rehm (1975) reported that depressed subjects do underestimate the amount of positive feedback they receive. Depressives might also selectively attend to the immediate (versus delayed) outcomes of their behavior. Such faulty self-monitoring would certainly interfere with the person's ability to sustain complex activities over extended periods of time or to work toward long-term goals.

Self-evaluation

The self-evaluative component of self-control involves a comparison between an estimate of behavioral performance as determined by self-monitoring and an internal standard of performance. Of course, the specific standards to be adopted can vary dramatically from person to person, and the characteristics of these standards can have important implications for interpersonal functioning. Rehm (1977) suggested that depressed persons probably adopt excessively stringent self-evaluative standards. By setting standards too high, they artificially rob themselves' of any successes. Potentially positive experiences are judged negatively because they fail to match some idealized criterion. A student might devalue a high grade, for instance, because it is not the highest grade in the class. The standards of depressed persons probably have an all-or-nothing flavor. If one does not perform incredibly well, then one has failed.

A second aspect of self-evaluation involves attribution of responsibility for behaviors or outcomes. Before a behavior can be meaningful compared to internal standards for performance, it must be *internally attributed*. In other words, the person must view the behavior as potentially under her or his own control. For a behavior to be positively evaluated, it must be internally attributed and judged to surpass performance standards. Similarly, for a behavior to be negatively evaluated, it must also be internally attributed but fail to meet performance standards.

Depressed persons are assumed to make one of two types of attributional errors. *First*, they make excessively internal attributions. Paired with overly stringent standards for performance, these attributions can lead the person to believe that positive outcomes are under his or her control but that he or she is incapable of attaining them. Rehm (1977) explained that the self-derogation and excessive guilt of some depressed persons would result from this combination of attributional and evaluative mayhem. *Second*, a depressed person makes excessively external attributions, that is, she or he believes that consequences are independent of performance. This point of view could contribute to the passivity and apathy so common to depression. In more recent explications of the self-control model of depression, O'Hara and Rehm (1983b) have described several additional attributional errors of depressed persons. These errors are derived from the theoretical relationship between learned helplessness and depression (Abramson, Seligman, & Teasdale, 1978).

Self-reinforcement

Self-control theory postulates that people reward their own behavior in much the same way that others reward them. Self-administration of rewarding and punishing consequences is said to supplement naturally occurring rewarding and punishing consequences in controlling behavior. Self-reinforcement occupies a particularly important role because it can maintain behavior in the absence of immediate external reinforcement. However, deficits in self-reinforcement (and excesses in self-punishment) might be central to depressive disorders. In a study reported by Rozensky and his associates (Rozensky, Rehm, Pry, & Roth, 1974), veterans administration hospital patients were given a word-recognition memory task. Although numbers of correct responses were the same, depressed patients gave themselves fewer self-rewards and more self-punishments than either mildly depressed or nondepressed patients. These findings have been replicated in a comparison of depressed and nondepressed college students (Roth, Rehm, & Rozensky, 1975).

Rehm (1977) suggested that low rates of behavior, infrequent response initiation, prolonged response latencies, and reduced persistence can be traced to deficits in self-reinforcement patterns. In the face of selective self-monitoring of negative events and stringent evaluative standards, high rates of self-punishment could further contribute to inhibition of adaptive responding.

To summarize, depression can be accounted for by six deficits in self-control: (a) selective self-monitoring for negative events, (b) selective self-monitoring for immediate rather than long-term consequences of behavior, (c) stringent self-evaluative standards, (d) inaccurate attributions, (e) deficient self-reinforcement, and (f) excessive self-punishment. Rehm and his associates developed a self-control treatment of depression based on these precepts. It has now been administered to individuals and groups of persons ranging from mildly to profoundly depressed. It is not our purpose to critically review its effectiveness, but several studies suggest it is indeed an effective approach to the treatment of depression (Fuchs & Rehm, 1977; Rehm, Fuchs, Roth, Kornblith, & Romano, 1979; Rehm et al., 1981; Roth, Bielski, Jones, Parker, & Osborn, 1982). Rehm's self-evaluation and self-reinforcement modules have been incorporated into social skills training, and their application will be described in later chapters.

EFFECTIVENESS OF SOCIAL SKILLS TRAINING

The treatment package described in this book has been subjected to several tests of its therapeutic effectiveness. Studies have been conducted or are currently underway that were designed to evaluate its effectiveness with outpatients whose depression is severe (Major Depressive Disorder) and chronic (Dysthymic Disorder). In this segment, we will describe the outcome of a large-scale study of the effectiveness of social skills training with female outpatients diagnosed as having Major Depressive Disorder (Bellack, Hersen, & Himmelhoch, 1983; Hersen et al., 1984).

One hundred and twenty of these female patients who sought treatment at the Western Psychiatric Institute and Clinic of the University of Pittsburgh School of Medicine were randomly assigned to one of four of the following individual treatment conditions.

Social skills training plus amitriptyline

Patients in this condition received 12 weekly 1-hour sessions of social skills training administered by an experienced clinical psychologist. They were also seen weekly by the medical staff for a 15–20 minute drug evaluation for the administration of amitriptyline (administered on a double-blind basis). Amitriptyline is a tricyclic antidepressant commonly used in the treatment of major depressive disorder. An initial dose of 50 mg/day was gradually increased to a maximum of 300 mg/day over a 4-week period.

In the 6-month period that followed, patients were seen for 6–8 additional sessions of social skills training and 6–8 additional drug evaluations. Social skills training sessions focused on problem solving and review. Dosages of amitriptyline were reduced, but not below 50 mg/day.

Social skills training plus placebo

Patients in this condition were treated identically to patients in the social skills training plus amitriptyline condition. However, they received pill placebos rather than amitriptyline. Placebo pills were physically identical to amitriptyline and were administered in double-blind fashion.

Amitriptyline

These patients received amitriptyline as described earlier. However, they received no social skills training.

Psychotherapy plus placebo

Patients in this condition received 12 weekly 1-hour sessions of time-limited psychodynamic psychotherapy during initial treatment and 6–8 additional sessions during the maintenance period. Psychotherapy was administered by an experienced clinical psychologist. Placebos were administered as described in the second condition.

Treatment outcome was assessed with a variety of self-report measures, clinician ratings of depression, and behavioral measures of social skill. First, we review the outcome for the behavioral measures as reported by Bellack et al. (1983). Before treatment, all patient groups performed more poorly than a normal comparison group on a role-play test of social skill. However, the treatment groups did not differ among themselves. After treatment, patients receiving social skills training (with amitripyline or placebo) showed the greatest improvement on this measure of social skill. Of all the patients, they appeared most similar to the normal, nondepressed women.

We now turn to the outcomes specifically related to the patients' depression (Hersen et al., 1984). Patients in all four treatment conditions showed significant and clinically meaningful improvements in their depression after treatment. Statistical tests showed that all groups improved, but none more than the others. That all treatments were effective and more or less equally so should be regarded as a plus for professionals attempting to treat seriously depressed individuals. No single treatment is effective with every patient, and we might need to combine several approaches or attempt several different procedures in sequential fashion to provide the best service to our clients.

An example of this viewpoint is raised by the literature on antidepressant medications. These medications are efficient to administer and can be very effective for many patients. However, they can have side effects that some patients are unable to tolerate, and some patients simply do not respond to medications. Therefore, it is important to provide alternative treatment procedures for patients who prefer a nonchemical approach or for whom antidepressants are ineffective. Social skills training can take its place among the tools of the seasoned clinician. In fact, Bellack et al. (1983) found that social skills training resulted in fewer dropouts and a higher proportion of completely remitted patients than the other procedures; thus it appears that patients found it to be a more palatable treatment, as well as a highly effective one.

The study on the treatment of patients diagnosed as having dysthymic disorder is currently underway. Preliminary results indicate outcomes similar to the Hersen et al. study (1984). In this study patients were randomly assigned to one of four treatments in a two (nortriptyline versus placebo) by two (social skills training versus crisis-supportive psychotherapy) factorial design. As of this date 68 subjects have been entered. Thirty-six have completed treatment. The outcome data on self-report and clinician ratings of depression for these 36 patients show statistically and clinically significant improvement for all four treatment combinations. This study also illustrates the effectiveness of social skills treatment, which is equal to the efficacy of nortriptyline.

In this chapter we have attempted to accomplish several goals. The reader should now be familiar with the theoretical bases for social skills training, the literature from which that support is derived, and the studies on the effectiveness of social skills training with major depressive and dysthymic patients. We now turn our attention to the next area of importance, the assessment of depression.

Chapter 3
Assessment of Depression

THE CONCEPT OF DEPRESSION

Most clinicians today are aware of the various controversies about the concept of depression. There are several proposed models of depression including biological (Whybrow, Akiskal, & McKinney, 1984), interpersonal (Klerman & Weissman, 1982), behavioral (Ferster, 1981; Lewinsohn, 1975), and cognitive (Rush & Beck, 1978; Garber & Seligman, 1980). Yet the most commonly employed concept of depression is the one embedded in the criteria of the Diagnostic and Statistical Manual of the American Psychiatric Association (DSM-III, 1980).

According to this approach, sets of correlated symptoms are amalgamated into a depressive syndrome. The concept of depression contains four sets of correlated symptoms that produce pain, impairment, or both in an individual. The painful symptoms comprise the *mood disturbance* aspect of the disorder and include sadness, irritability, and loss of pleasure. Disturbances in *somatic functioning* constitute the second area of symptoms and include appetite and sleep disturbance. *Behavioral symptoms* include crying, agitation or retardation, and general decrease in activity. *Cognitive symptoms* include feelings of worthlessness and guilt, fatigue, and difficulties with memory and focusing of attention. The process of diagnosis and measurement of depression has generally evolved from this syndrome concept. The net result is that most diagnostic procedures and measurement strategies in use today have been derived from the syndromal conceptual model. Rather than debate whether this is an appropriate model, we shall present the techniques commonly in use.

DIAGNOSIS OF DEPRESSION

From the standpoint of recognition or diagnosis of depression, much progress has been made in the last 10 years. Endicott and Spitzer (1978) have produced several structured clinical interview schedules designed to reliably

15

arrive at a diagnosis of depression. The Schedule for Affective Disorders and Schizophrenia (SADS) (Endicott & Spitzer, 1978) is currently the most widely used instrument. This interviewer guide exists in two forms: the SADS, which focuses on a current episode of a disorder; and the SADS-L (lifetime version), which provides historical data about the patient and the time course of previous episodes. Both guides are used in conjunction with the Research Diagnostic Criteria (RDC) (Spitzer, Endicott, & Robins, 1978), which is the forerunner of the DSM-III (APA, 1980).

These instruments, in the hands of a trained interviewer, are used to arrive at a diagnosis on the basis of a 60–90 minute interview. They have been shown to have high interrater agreement for the presence of major depressive disorder (Spitzer, Endicott, & Robins, 1977). RDC and DSM-III criteria are not identical. One of the areas in which they differ is the nosology of less severe depression, which is referred to as dysthymic disorder in the DSM-III. This category roughly corresponds to the former *neurotic depression*. The RDC defines two syndromes that are subsumed under the dysthymic label of DSM-III: intermittent depressive disorder and minor depressive disorder. The case examples employed in this volume are clients diagnosed according to the RDC as having intermittent or minor depression.

When we conduct a SADS interview we usually videotape the entire procedure, which allows us to replay it if we have unanswered questions and also assists us in establishing the reliability of the diagnosis. For a clinician interested in establishing the correct diagnosis, less arduous procedures would be warranted. Under these circumstances the clinician might wish to audiotape the interview and later score the SADS (or SADS-L) by reviewing the audio record. Readers interested in the more rigorous procedures are referred to a paper by Gibbon, McDonald-Scott, and Endicott (1981).

The clinician should think of the SADS as a helpful guide and not as a lockstep procedure. Over the course of our work, we have conducted many SADS-L interviews and found that there are some patients who have answered *no* to the initial screening questions; yet, when we have pursued this area anyway (in violation of the interview guide), we have uncovered important information from a reluctant patient. Not surprisingly, these areas of reluctance usually involve some personal embarrassment regarding sexuality or substance use. We have found additional information about such issues as abortions, homosexuality, and children given up for adoption. Some of this information is related to the depressed mood and can change the diagnosis. We have pursued this additional information in order to lessen the number of *surprises* uncovered later in treatment that could significantly alter the course and content of sessions.

Probably the most difficult distinction the clinician will have to make as a result of the SADS interview is differentiating dysthymic disorder from major depressive disorder. Little work has been done comparing these two diagnostic groups on commonly employed scales used to assess depression. Our work with dysthymic disorder in comparison with major depressive disorder (Gansler, Heimberg, & Becker, 1985) has attempted to do this. Patients diagnosed as having intermittent or minor depressive disorder by the SADS-L, RDC procedure were compared with patients diagnosed as having major depressive disorder on their response patterns on the Hamilton Rating Scale for Depression (HRSD) (Hamilton, 1967) and the Beck Depression Inventory (BDI) (A.T. Beck, Ward, Mendelsohn, Mock, & Erbaugh, 1961). Major depressive patients were rated as significantly more depressed on the HRSD and significantly higher on somatic anxiety, gastrointestinal distress, weight loss, paranoia, depressed mood, and suicide potential. Dysthymics were rated significantly higher for increased appetite. The two diagnostic groups were not significantly different on the overall BDI, but four individual items were significantly different. Major depressives reported more loss of appetite and associated weight loss, whereas dysthymics reported more lack of satisfaction and fatigue. Further analysis of the Endogenomorphy subscale of the HRSD developed by Thase, Hersen, Bellack, Himmelhoch, and Kupfer (1983) revealed that major depressive patients scored significantly higher M = 8.33, than dysthymic patients, M = 5.67, $t(22) = 2.88$, $p < 0.01$.

These data imply that the BDI might not be able to distinguish between the two diagnostic categories, but the HRSD might be more sensitive. Major-depressive-disorder clients are more likely to display higher symptom levels in the areas of mood disturbance and somatic functioning, whereas the intermittent- and minor-depressive-disorder clients are more likely to display higher levels of cognitive symptoms.

MEASUREMENT OF THE SEVERITY OF DEPRESSION

There are several self-report and clinical rating scales with established reliability and validity in the measurement of the severity of depressive disorder. These scales differ in the emphasis they place on particular aspects of the depressive symptom constellation. Some draw more heavily from the somatic domain, whereas others draw more from cognitive symptoms. But most have developed under the syndromal conceptualization of depression described earlier, and therefore they attempt to at least sample from the four domains outlined.

Self-Report Scales

Subjective experiences are an integral component of depression and can only be assessed by the patient's self-report. Self-report scales attempt to assess these subjective reactions and attitudes that make up a central component of the depressive experience. Though these scales contribute only personal, subjective information, they are, nonetheless, important aspects of depression.

Beck Depression Inventory

The most commonly employed instrument is the BDI (A. T. Beck et al., 1961). It consists of 21 items designed to measure depressed mood over the previous 7 days, each with four response alternatives rated from *none* (0) to *high* (3), depending on the severity of depression. Scoring is easily accomplished by adding each item score and deriving a simple total. Scale items sample the range of depressive symptoms patients experience, with somewhat more items drawn from cognitive than behavioral or somatic symptoms. Abut 50% of the items reflect negative thoughts such as "I am a complete failure as a person" or "I feel discouraged about the future." Roughly 15% of the items reflect behavioral manifestations of depression, such as "I have lost most of my interest in other people" or "I cry all the time now." The remaining items reflect the somatic symptoms of depression, with items such as "My appetite is much worse now" and "I have lost more than 5 pounds."

Interpretation of the scores is as follows: 0–10, healthy mental state; 11–18, mild to moderate depression; 19–29, moderate depression; 29–63, moderate to severe depression. A split-half reliability of 0.93 has been reported by A. T. Beck et al. (1961), and independent clinical judgment of depression has been shown to relate well to BDI scores by several investigators (A. T. Beck et al., 1961; Metcalfe & Goldman, 1965; Williams, Barlow, & Agras, 1972).

The Depression Adjective Checklist (DACL)

This instrument is popular with clinicians and clinical researchers for use as a quick measure of depressed mood. The scale is designed to measure depressed mood within the previous 24 hours. It requires the patient to select from a list of 14 adjectives those that best reflect his or her current mood. Administration is quick and convenient, but scoring is more complex. Each selected adjective that expresses a depressed tone contributes one point toward the total score, and each adjective not selected that expresses a happy mood contributes one point. This last procedure means that errors of omission by a patient count toward higher ratings of depression. Examples of adjectives indicative of depressed mood are *downhearted, unhappy, glum, sorrowful,* and *heavy hearted.* Adjectives that reflect a happy tone include *clean, hopeful, alive, bright,* and *lively.* Scores are interpreted as follows: normal, 3–5; nondepressed patients, 4–6; depressed patients, 7+. The DACL has seven different forms divided into two groups. Forms A, B, C, D have 14 items each, and forms E, F, G have 17 items each. In total there are 72 adjectives that describe depressed mood and 36 adjectives that describe normal or happy mood. Correlations among different forms of the DACL range from 0.83 to 0.91, whereas the various DACL forms correlate with several other self-report measures of depression and are sensitive to treatment effects (Lubin, 1981).

Hopkins Symptom Checklist

This instrument has existed in several forms with the 35- and 58-item (HSCL) versions being quite common. More recently, the 90-item version (HSCL-90) has been routinely employed to assess a number of dimensions of psychopathology. Historically this measurement system was derived from the Discomfort Scale (Parloff, Kelman, & Frank, 1954), whose origins are traceable to the Cornell Medical Index.

The current 90-item version still requests patients to rate, "How much were you bothered by" for each type of symptom. The 90-item self-administered scale requires rating each item on a 5-point scale as follows: *not at all* (0), *a little bit* (1), *moderately* (2), *quite a bit* (3) and *extremely* (4). An attempt was made to keep the vocabulary content equal for all items by restricting item content to simple phrases and commonly used words. The HCSL-90 contains 9 subscales derived by factor analysis as follows: (a) somatization, (b) obsessive–compulsive, (c) interpersonal sensitivity, (d) depression, (e) anxiety, (f) hostility, (g) phobic anxiety, (h) paranoid ideation, (i) psychoticism. Scoring of each subscale is accomplished by summing the 0 to 4 possible points assigned to each item within a factor subscale and then dividing this total score by the number of questions in the factor. Three global scores are calculated from the factor scores. *First*, a grand sum of all the item scores is created by addition. *Next*, this grand sum is divided by the total number of items (in this case 90), yielding an average score per item. *Last*, a positive index is created by dividing the grand sum by the number of items with a score greater than 1. Interpretation of these global scores is as follows: grand total, normal under 18; clinical pathology, greater than 40; average score per item, under 1.0; positive index, under 2.0. Generally, scores on each factor under 1.0 are normal. Extensive data are available about the factor structure and the sensitivity of the instrument to pharmacological treatment interventions (Derogatis, Lipman, & Covi, 1973).

In our work we have employed the 58-item version (HSCL-58), and the scoring for this scale is somewhat different. First, there are only five factors, as opposed to the nine factors of the 90-item version. These factors are depression, obsessive–compulsive, interpersonal sensitivity, anxiety, and somatization. Each item is scored on a 4-point, as opposed to a 5-point scale, as follows: *not at all* (1), *a little* (2), *quite a bit* (3), and *extremely* (4). The cutoff score on a factor for clinically significantly pathology is greater than 2.0, as opposed to greater than 1.0 on the 90-item version.

Zung Self-Rating Depression Scale

Most clinicians have heard about the Zung scale (Zung, 1974) although few have actually administered it. The scale consists of 20 items requiring a patient to endorse one of four frequencies of occurrence ranging from *none or little of the time* to *all or most of the time*. Ten items are worded symptomatically positive and 10 symptomatically negative. Scoring is accomplished by addition of the 1 to 4 possible points for each item, and this sum is then divided by the highest possible score (80). This quotient is rounded to the nearest integer and multiplied by 100. Score range is 20 at the lowest and 100 at the most extreme.

Zung (1967) provided norms and suggested cutoff scores for ranges of depression. These norms suggest that nondepressed persons score around 33. Depressed persons tend to score above 50, with a mean of 74. After treatment, depressed outpatients show a decline from 74 to 39. Items sample from four symptom areas: pervasive mood disturbances, physiological disturbances, psychomotor (behavioral) disturbances, and psychological (cognitive) disturbances. Some items are: "I feel downhearted and blue," "I notice that I'm losing weight," "I have trouble with constipation." Split-half reliability is 0.73, and the scale correlates significantly with clinician ratings of pathology and the BDI. In comparison with those on the BDI, the Zung items are more frequently drawn from behavioral and somatic symptom constellations.

Clinician Rating Scales

Scales of this type are administered by a trained clinician in an interview format. Most scales require a structured interview, with the clinician asking questions taken directly from the scale and then rating the responses, proceeding in this fashion until the last item has been answered. A notable exception to this rule are two scales: the Global Assessment Scale (Endicott, Spitzer, Fleiss, & Cohen, 1976) and the Raskin Global Severity of Depression Scale (Raskin, Schulterbrandt, Reatig, & Rice, 1967).

Global Assessment Scale

The GAS is a rating scale used to evaluate the functioning of a patient over the previous week. Scale values range from 1 (the lowest level of functioning) to 100 for healthy and happy persons. Each 10-point range is anchored with a description of the level of functioning and psychopathology, but theoretically the rater can assign any score from 1 to 100. The two highest intervals (81–90, 91–100) are for those individuals without significant psychopathology and with many positive signs of mental health such as a wide range of interests, social effectiveness, warmth, and integrity. The interval between 71 and 80 is for individuals with no or minimal psychopathology but without the positive mental health features. Most people above 70 would not seek assistance for psychological difficulty. Most outpatients range between 31 to 70, whereas most inpatients vary between 1 and 40.

The GAS was developed from the Health–Sickness Rating Scale (Luborsky, 1962) and has much in common with its predecessor. After an unstructured clinical interview, the clinician examines the GAS for the anchor interval that best describes the patient's functioning and then assigns a score within that anchor range, to give a finer gradation. Reliability of the GAS scale ranges from a low of 0.69 to a high of 0.76 using intraclass correlations and independent raters conducting sequential interviews. When more than one rater observed the same interview, the intraclass correlation rose to 0.91. The GAS correlates moderately with independently rated measures of overall severity of psychopathology, is related to the recurrence of symptoms, and is sensitive to therapeutically induced change (Endicott et al., 1976).

Raskin Global Severity of Depression Scale

The RGSD is a three-item scale assessing the patient's verbal report of mood, behavior implying sadness, and secondary symptoms of depression (cognitive). Each of the three items is rated on a 5-point scale ranging from *not at all* to *very much*. Scores range from no symptoms (3) to very much symptomatic (15), and a score of 7 to 9 is an indication of moderate depression. The scale is scored subsequent to a general, unstructured, clinical interview.

The Raskin scale was developed in the context of a colloborative clinical research study examining pharmacological treatment of major depressive disorder sponsored by the National Institute of Mental Health. An attempt was made to extract a scale that would be treatment responsive and representative of the major facets of depressive psychopathology. The Raskin scale was derived from the 41-item Inventory of Psychic and Somatic Complaints (IPSC) (Parloff et al., 1954), which in turn is a modification of the Symptom Distress Scale (Frank, Gliedman, Imber, Nash, & Stone, 1957). The IPSC was administered to 124 hospitalized patients, and a factor analysis was carried out on the data (Raskin et al., 1967). Later, a larger sample was examined, with the same factors resulting (Raskin, Schulterbrandt, Reatig, &

McKeon, 1969). The three items now on the RAS result from these analyses and are treatment responsive and reflective of the psychopathology of depression.

Hamilton Rating Scale for Depression

The original HRSD (Hamilton, 1960) contains 17 items selected to sample from mood and cognitive, behavioral, and somatic symptoms of depression. The more recent editions have expanded from 21 to 24 and then to 26 items, to include more items from the cognitive domain. Each of the versions is administered by a trained clinician following a structured interview format.

A recent study by O'Hara and Rehm (1983a) demonstrated that high levels of agreement can be obtained by clinical psychology doctoral students. The original data on reliability were restricted to psychiatrists as interviewers. Individual items are scored on a 0–3 or 1–4 scale, depending on the version used, and a total score is the sum of these scores. Thase et al. (1983) suggested items 5–9, 16, 18, and 23 be used as indications of endogeneous depression. This endogeneity subscale consists primarily of items measuring somatic changes associated with depression, such as insomnia in the middle of the night or early morning, fatigue, slowing of speech rate, obvious signs of agitation, loss of weight, decrease in appetite, and helplessness. The Hamilton scale has been used extensively in the evaluation of depressed patients, and consequently a good deal is known about it. It has acceptably high reliability, is treatment sensitive (Bech, 1981; Hedlund & Vieweg, 1979), and has become a standard rating scale for use with affective-disorder patients.

CASE EXAMPLE

We have selected one of our former patients as a typical example of the application of social skills training to dysthymic disorder. We shall use this one patient as an example in many chapters of this book, so that the reader can follow the progress of a patient through the entire diagnostic, social skill assessment, and treatment process. To give the reader a fuller picture of this patient, we provide a summary of the initial SADS interview.

Patient name: S. J.
Age: 37
Marital status: single, one child (a son, age 5)

Presenting Problem
Ms. S. J. is currently employed as an assistant manager with a local corporation. She lives in an apartment with her son. She reports long periods of depression, which she assumes are related to her menstrual cycle. She claims to be more depressed at particular times every month, but this pattern is not always

consistent. Her dissatisfaction and dysphoria are consistent and constant, but her reactions to her mood vary. About one half of the time she "looks to religion" and goes to church; the other half results in social withdrawal, lack of interest, and tearful episodes. She finds herself contemplating suicide but has never taken any action on these thoughts. She often thinks, "I wish I were dead" or "I wish the Lord would take me." These thoughts occurred most recently before major surgery, which she viewed as a perfect opportunity to die.

Ms. S. J. describes herself as lonely, sad, isolated, and lacking any interest in usual activities, such as going to movies or sports. She has few social contacts, blames herself for her present condition, and frequently worries about her loneliness and her finances. She often disconnects her telephone to avoid contact with her friends.

Interview Behavior

Ms. S. J. is an attractive, neatly dressed woman, who was cooperative and coherent throughout the interview. During the interview she cried frequently, especially when her child was discussed. She feels that her somber moods affect her child and make her a poor mother.

Relevant Social History

Ms. S. J. is originally from this community, and her parents and three siblings live nearby. She feels that her family is helpful and supportive.

Several years ago she took a job that required her to move. During this stay away from her family she became pregnant and later gave birth to her son. She describes the father as a casual acquaintance with whom she desires no further contact.

Shortly after these events, she decided to return to her home in this area to rear her son. Since returning home, she has continued to be depressed. On occasion she has dated again, but she feels that no one would be seriously interested in her.

Psychiatric History

She has neither sought nor received any previous mental health treatment. There does not appear to be evidence of a family history of depression.

Diagnosis

Based on the SADS-L interview and the RDC, she was given a diagnosis of *Intermittent Depressive Disorder*. The SADS-L yielded the following data about her depression:

1. She has continued to be depressed over the course of the last 4 years.
2. She experiences 2–3 days of depression and then experiences 2–3 days when she is partly relieved of this feeling. She can experience one or several days of good mood, but has not had periods of good mood lasting longer than a few weeks. She has not missed work time because of her mood, nor has she let her mood interfere with her parenting.
3. She does not report a sleep disturbance or appetite disturbance. She denies fatigue but does admit to lack of interest. She does feel down on herself but denies having trouble concentrating or making decisions. She does admit to thoughts of suicide but has not made any attempt.
4. She admits that she has bouts of crying, broods about unpleasant events that have happened, and feels inadequate and pessimistic.
5. She has sought treatment for her depression from her family doctor, who referred her here.

Chapter 4

Assessment of Social Skill

Successful and efficient application of the techniques of social skills training is partly dependent on the assessment of social skills. In this chapter we will briefly describe several issues involved in the assessment of social skill. Subsequent to this preparatory information, we will describe the framework we use in understanding social skill. In this section we present the various components of this framework and provide the reader with specific behavioral referents. From here, we turn to assessment procedures *per se*, covering the techniques of clinical interviewing, brief role-play assessment, extended role-play assessment, self-monitoring and self-report, including homework assignments. To integrate each of these techniques into the framework of social skill presented earlier, we describe the kind of information each technique should provide. Throughout this presentation we inject clinical case material as examples. We now turn to our first section, delineating the major issues in the assessment of social skill.

MAJOR ISSUES

Exactly what constitutes "social skill?" This elusive question has led clinicians and researchers in various directions. As a result of their writings, a number of important issues have been raised. We will highlight the seven issues most important for social skill assessment.

1. Skill deficits versus anxiety and cognitions.
2. Response consequences versus response quality.
3. Situational control versus individual differences.
4. Static versus dynamic control of social behavior.
5. Performance-class independence versus generalization.
6. Natural reinforcement versus punishment.
7. Molar versus molecular measurement.

The reader desiring a more comprehensive discussion of these areas is referred to a recent review by Becker and Heimberg (in press). We now turn to a brief discussion of each of these seven key issues.

Skill Deficits Versus Anxiety and Cognitions

We can directly observe poor social performance. The reasons for this poor performance have traditionally been divided into two major explanatory variables. The *skills deficit assumption* presumes that individuals always perform to the best of their ability and that performance failure results from lack of the behavioral competencies necessary for proper performance, that is, "a social skills deficit."

In fact, poor social performance can result from a number of factors including negative self-evaluations, anxiety, and inadequate knowledge of social norms. *Anxiety* and *negative self-evaluations* are presumed to inhibit the display of skillful social behavior. Consequently, evaluation of poor social performance should attend to both skill deficits and inhibitory factors.

Response Consequences Versus Response Quality

One way of judging the adequacy of social performance is by its effectiveness. Did the performance actually produce the desired outcome? Libet and Lewinsohn defined social skill as "the complex ability to maximise the rate of positive reinforcement and to minimize the strength of punishment from others" (1973, p. 311). Such a definition places emphasis on the efficacy of the performance.

A response can be effective even if it violates accepted social norms (for example, physical threats); thus a contrasting perspective on social skill emphasizes the quality of the performance. A skilled response must conform to social norms and contain the correct amounts of the subcomponents (for example, eye contact, voice tone) that make up the overall performance. The more "correct" components contained in the response, the more skillful it is assumed to be. However, just because a behavior is well performed does not mean it will produce the desired consequences.

Situational Control Versus Individual Differences

Environmental variables are assumed to play a vital role in the control of social behavior. Social skill is not considered a general personality trait but is presumed to change, depending on contextual variables. Individual components and the overall quality of a performance can vary as a function of changes in the situation.

In addition to situational control, there are significant individual differences in skill. Thus there is definitely some consistency across situations. Individuals can be stratified as being more or less skillful generally, and predictions can be made about differences in performance between highly skilled and less skilled individuals.

Static Versus Dynamic Control of Social Behavior

Early studies aimed at demonstrating the effects of situational variables found potent effects for these factors. For example, Eisler, Hersen, Miller, and Blanchard (1975) employed role-play assessments that varied in terms of sex and familiarity of the role-play partner. Performances of the patients differed dramatically as a function of these contextual parameters. This line of investigation continued to conceptualize the influence of contextual factors in this "one application, one effect" style. For example, the familiarity of an interaction partner would have a consistent effect on social behavior and would not vary as the interaction varied.

More recent studies have conceptualized a different type of contextual variable, which is thought of as fluctuating over the course of an interpersonal interaction and, therefore, producing variable effects depending on the time of assessment. For example, Faraone and Hurtig (1985) conducted a temporal analysis of a 15-minute interaction between men and women. Less anxious (and presumably more socially skilled) men, in comparison with more highly anxious men, were more verbal, talked more about themselves, talked for longer intervals about themselves, and assisted their partners more often when they appeared to be "stuck." Additionally, these men made more positive evaluations of conversational topics and were less likely to initiate negative topics. This study points to dynamic variables as potent influences on social behavior.

Performance-class Independence Versus Generalization

Do social skills acquired to cope with one kind of interpersonal situation assist in learning another set of skills useful in another type of situation? Early investigation of this question (McFall & Lillesand, 1971) suggested little effect from learning one type of skill on better or faster acquisition of another type of skill. More recent work (St. Lawrence, Hughes, Goff, & Palmer, 1983) has suggested that there is transfer, and skill acquisition in one area can aid acquisition or performance in another area.

Natural Reinforcement Versus Punishment

An assumption inherent in social skills treatment is positive correlation between a better quality of social performance and a more positive outcome for the client. In short, positive reinforcement would naturally accrue to a better trained client. Kelly, Kern, Kirkley, Patterson, and Keane (1980) examined the consequences of handling mistreatment with a good-quality assertive response. Persons carrying out such skilled behavior were seen as more competent but less flexible, less likable, and less warm. Further, females employing these skills were evaluated more negatively than their male counterparts.

This study suggests that an assumption of naturally occurring positive reinforcement is not always tenable, and, in fact, naturally occurring punishment can occur. These data suggest that social skill training include an empathic component. Further, homework assignments should be done carefully, in order to not diminish the positive qualities of interpersonal attraction.

One final point. Clients will be able to provide a history of previous behaviors and the punishments or reinforcements contingent upon them. This history is important for two reasons. *First*, it provides a history of the interpersonal partner's previous behavior and a prediction about how such a person will respond in the future. *Second*, a client's willingness to try new behaviors with such a person can be effected by past experience.

Molar Versus Molecular Measurement

Two approaches to the assessment of social performance have appeared in the scientific literature. One approach, labeled the *molar approach*, consists of judgments made by raters on global Likert-type scales. For example, a rater could be asked to judge the overall social skill of a patient on a 7-point scale with anchors ranging from poorly skilled to highly skilled. The second approach is labeled *molecular* and consists of breaking down a performance into its subcomponents and then rating each subcomponent on more objective scales. For example, a social performance might be broken down into latency to respond (measured in seconds), duration of response, gaze, number of speech disturbances, number of smiles, and so on. Molecular ratings such as these provide useful information to aid in modifying a response. These individual components are not always highly intercorrelated and are only moderately correlated with global ratings of social skill. Molar ratings appear to be more highly correlated to overall social competence but do not provide enough specific information to plan treatment.

SOCIAL SKILL: A FRAMEWORK

Our framework of social skill consists of six key areas that derive from the seven issues just touched upon. We assess each of these areas in different ways, which we will describe next. Beyond the assessment itself, these areas provide a basis for organizing the treatment interventions we discuss in the subsequent chapters. We now turn to a description of each area.

Molecular Assessments and Skill Deficits

To formulate specific treatment targets, we have chosen a molecular assessment strategy and a molar assessment. We obtain one molar measure of overall skill judged on a 5-point Likert-type scale. Most of our effort is concentrated on the molecular components, to be described.

This assessment is carried out on a standard set of 12 role-play scenes, included in the Appendix. Clients are introduced to the assessment through a description of the link between social performance and depression. Further, because interpersonal skill is the focus of treatment, clients are told that this assessment will aid in sharpening the treatment focus and effectiveness. All 12 scenes are videotaped and later reviewed and scored by assistants according to the criteria in Tables 4.1 and 4.2. We prepare our clients by describing the role-play assessment format. Then we review the 12 scenes with them and insert the names of 12 real people who fit the category. After that, we give final instructions and try one practice scene to make sure the clients carry out the role plays properly.

We presume that difficulties revealed by these assessments constitute legitimate targets for therapy.

Dynamic Control of Social Behavior

We presume that dynamic factors exert important influences over the display of social behavior and that truly skillful behavior requires the client to continually attend to these sources of information and to modify social responding "on the fly" in order to be responsive to these fluctuating stimuli. Table 4.3 shows dynamic factors we assess. Because role-play assessments do not allow the repeated interchanges of actual interpersonal interaction, we carry out extended role-play assessments during the first few therapy sessions. During these assessments the therapist can tailor scenes to a specific client and can add nuances not available in the standard series. This more fluid format is better suited for assessing the dynamic stimuli listed in Table 4.3.

Situational Control of Social Behavior

We have tried to distinguish between two sets of contextual factors that affect social behavior. The first set we labeled *dynamic factors* and the second *situational*. Situational factors exert an influence but do not change over the course of an interaction. Table 4.4 presents situational factors we assess.

Table 4.1
Molecular Components of Social Skill and Their Ratings

1. Loudness
   a. Inaudible/extremely loud all or most of the time.
   b. Inaudible/extremely loud some of the time.
   c. Moderate appropriate loudness.
2. Latency
   Use an electronic stopwatch that can record elapsed and total time. Start timing at the instant the role-play prompter finishes speaking, and stop the lap time as soon as the client utters her or his first word.
3. Duration
   Record, using the lap/total time watch above. Press the lap-time button to record this time in memory, but let the watch continue to run as the subject continues to speak. At the moment the subject stops speaking stop the watch, giving total time, that is latency and duration added together. Duration is calculated by subtracting latency from total elapsed time. Pauses longer than 3 sec are subtracted from duration times.
4. Smiles
   a. No smiles.
   b. At least one smile in the target scene.
5. Speech disturbances
   Count all instances of um, er, oh, ah.
   Do not count words such as well, but and other words with conversational value.
   a. At least one occurrence.
   b. No occurrence or no response.
6. Affect
   a. Very flat, unemotional tone of voice with an audiotaped example provided.
   b. Moderate intonation with taped example.
   c. Full, lively intonation with a taped example.
7. Gaze
   a. Focal point of the eyes is on the face of the interaction partner at least 33% of the time regardless of head orientation.
   b. Eye contact as described between 33% and 66% of the time.
   c. Eye contact as described, more than 66% of the time.

Response Quality and Cognitions

This aspect of social behavior focuses on two parts of social performance that are related to one another. The first part is the actual social performance displayed by the client. The second part consists of those aspects of the performance attended to by the client, how these parts were evaluated, and what self-generated consequences were assigned to the performance. We presume that the client is already using some system of attending to and evaluating the quality of her or his behavior and using the results of this evaluation to apply self-reinforcement or punishment. During the course of our assessments, we try to determine what cognitive system is currently in place, as a basis for making modifications.

Table 4.2
Molar Evaluation of Social Skill and Its Rating

1. Positive Assertion
Verbal content of the client after receiving positive behavior from the partner such as a compliment or a favor.
All ratings are done on the words spoken, without regard to intonation or timing, which have already been rated as a molecular component.
a. Minimal response – subject says nothing or mumbles.
b. Responds but denies the positive nature of the event; for example, "That's not much help." or "Really, I don't think so."
c. Responds with partial agreement or acknowledgement and self-derogatory statement, such as "Thank you, but I don't deserve it."
d. Agrees or acknowledges without a derogatory or a positive statement in return such as, "Thank you."
e. Acknowledges or agrees and returns a positive statement, such as, "Thank you, its nice of you to do that. I hope I can return the favor sometime."
2. Negative Assertion
Verbal content of the client after receiving negative behavior from the partner such as an unreasonable request.
a. Accepts criticism or unfair treatment without objection or does not respond.
b. Accepts criticism or unfair treatment with implausible explanation or poor excuse, such as, "OK, but I might feel bad." "Yes, other people probably see that too."
c. Responds equivocally exemplified by difficulty in assessing what the person is trying to communicate, but does not accept criticism or unfair treatment; for example, "I'll see" or "What would you do?"
d. Does not accept the criticism or unfair treatment and makes comments, returns criticism, or expresses annoyance without an explanation or with an evasive explanation? For example, "No, I don't want to" or "No, it's not my problem."
e. Does not accept the criticism or unfair treatment and responds with a direct explanation and a request for a future change or an agreement for a future change; for example, "I don't agree with that because I've been a good worker" or "I think your criticism is unfair, so let me explain."

Table 4.3
Dynamic Stimuli Involved in Social Behavior

1. *Floor shifts.* Cues to indicate change from speaker to listener or vice versa.
2. *Topic changes.* Changes from one related line of conversation to another line.
3. *Clarifying others' communications.* Restatements of others' messages to clarify meaning.
4. *Persistence.* Cues indicating that the other person is ambivalent such as "Maybe. I'll think about it."
5. *Detection of partner's emotion.* Changes in voice volume, pitch, or speech rate. Changes in facial expression and eye contact, flushing, widened eyes, and changes in muscle tone. Changes in intensity of gestures or speed of movement. Abrupt floor shifts or topic changes.
6. *Reinforcement or punishment from the partner.* Offers of future reinforcement or punishments.
7. *Recall of past interactions.* The history of past reinforcement and punishment provides information about the likelihood of particular behaviors being well received or not.
8. *Unpredicted responses from others.* Anger, affection, or indifference, for example, insults or a romantic embrace.

Table 4.4
Situational Factors in Social Behavior

1. Human Characteristics
   a. Sex of the interaction partner.
   b. Age of the partner, for example, child versus adult.
   c. Superordinate versus subordinate social roles.
   d. Less ability versus greater ability, for example, impaired intellectual ability, poor hearing, an impairing illness.
   e. Friends versus strangers.
   f. Intimates versus strangers or friends.
2. Setting Characteristics
   a. Work.
   b. Home.
   c. Public places such as restaurants.
   d. Within transportation systems – trains planes, cars, buses.
   e. Within communications networks, telephones, computers.
   f. Recreational settings, pools, saunas, gymnasiums.

Performance Class Independence

We have embraced the assumption that performance classes are independent and, therefore, do not presume that training in one class necessarily aids training in another class. This assumption is embodied in our hierarchical approach to treatment and assessment. We divide social behavior into three performance classes.

1. *Positive assertion:* behaviors that have a positive impact on the social interaction partner. Examples from this class commonly addressed in treatment are offering to do a favor for another, yielding to the other's request, displaying physical or verbal affection, treating another fairly, and displaying respect for another.
2. *Negative assertion:* behaviors that have a negative impact on the social interaction partner. Common examples from this class include refusing a request from the other, not offering a favor, removing resources given or lent to the other, requesting less future behavior, and ignoring the other.
3. *Conversational skill:* behaviors that allow the client to initiate, maintain, and end conversations. These skills emphasize exchange of information without a positive or negative consequence for either member of the dyad.

Response Consequences and Natural Reinforcement/ Punishment

We have presumed that naturally occurring reinforcement and punishment are not sufficient to support the new skills we have recently trained without a more systematic approach. In our assessments we attempt to obtain information about the characteristics of the "natural" environment to which the client must return. Our treatment strategy includes planned attempts to increase the reinforcements naturally available and to avoid the punishments. Exactly how we carry out our assessments to obtain the desired information is our next topic.

ASSESSMENT PROCEDURES

Clinical Interviewing

Although advances in objective assessment are desired, there is, as yet, no other assessment technique that can attain the breadth and subtlety of a clinical interview. Historical events of the patients' life can only be obtained from her or him, and it is often the case that the objective event alone is not nearly so important as the meaning of this event to the individual. This kind of self-report information can only be obtained by the interview process. Our clinical interview serves to obtain information about:

1. The history of reinforcement and punishment from others.
2. The client's self-reported perception of consequences of certain social behaviors and evaluation of the natural reinforcement and punishment history.
3. Situational control factors.
4. The client's employment of self-evaluation and self-reinforcement for social behavior.
5. The client's perceived difficulties with the performance classes of positive and negative assertion and conversational skill.
6. Mood and how different social events and social behaviors covary with it.

We start with a general inquiry into the historical developments of the patients' chief complaints and continue in the pursuit of factors important in the control of social behavior (situational control, dynamic control, performance-class independence, reinforcement, punishment, self-evaluations, and so on). Once this general information has been acquired, we focus on the present and the recent past and carry out a checklist assessment. Table 4.5 presents a summary of our checklist, which is similar to that of Galassi and Galassi (1977).

When the patient reports difficulty with a particular performance class in a certain situation and with certain types of people, we ask him or her to rate, on a 1–100 scale, the difficulty of carrying out the performance with this person. We proceed in this fashion until all the categories have been assessed. At this point we ask the patient to reexamine his or her listing and to make

Table 4.5
Checklist of Factors Involved in Social Behavior

1. *Human characteristics.* People with whom the client potentially has difficulty.
   a. Friends of the same sex.
   b. Friends of the opposite sex.
   c. Bosses or supervisors of the same sex.
   d. Bosses or supervisors of the opposite sex.
   e. Professionals of the same sex – doctors, lawyers.
   f. Professionals of the opposite sex.
   g. Salesmen or saleswomen, waiters or waitresses.
   h. Coworkers or colleagues of the same sex.
   i. Coworkers or colleagues of the opposite sex.
   j. Father or father-in-law.
   k. Mother or mother-in-law.
   l. Spouse, lover, boyfriend or girlfriend.
   m. Children.
2. *Situational factors.* Static contextual factors that influence social behavior.
   a. At work, school.
   b. At home.
   c. Public places.
   d. Within transportation systems.
   e. Within communication systems.
   f. In recreational settings.
3. *Performance classes.* These might be problematic.
   a. Positive assertion.
   b. Negative assertion.
   c. Conversational interaction.

final comparisons in the ordering, so that we eventually end with a rank ordering of performance classes and people arranged in order of the patient's reported level of difficulty. This process is difficult for both patient and clinician and can often consume 2 therapy hours. Problematic situations usually cluster around certain people and types of performance classes or situations. We do not have reliability and validity data associated with our assessment, but we do proceed one step further by using this data to move into behavioral simulations of the problematic scenes, to allow the clinician a closer and more natural look at the behavior in question.

The reader should be aware that the interview, although highly valuable, is an inexact process. Bias can be introduced from the faulty recall of the patient, from the patient's poor recognition of her or his own behavior, or from the patient's desire to simply withhold vital information. The interviewer might fail to pursue adequate detail or fail to cover important areas.

We try to maintain accuracy and completeness not only by obtaining historical and self-report information but also by observing the patient's behavior in the interview. These observations can confirm the self-report information just given by the client or cause the clinician to be suspicious about the accuracy of the self-report. These clinical hunches often serve as the basis of role-play assessments involving situations in which the client reports no difficulty. In this way we try to obviate some of the difficulties of the interview process.

Role-Play Assessment

One of the cardinal assumptions of behavioral assessment is that direct observation of behavior is the most valid and desirable strategy. Such direct observation of natural behavior is usually not ethical or practical. We have chosen simulations as the next best thing to direct observation. Our 12 simulations are carried out with an assistant and are aimed at assessment of the molecular components of behavior listed in Table 4.1. Scene content and procedure are adapted from earlier work with depressed clients (Bellack et al., 1983).

The scenes are divided into three dichotomous categories: scenes requiring negative versus positive assertion, a more familiar versus a less familiar interaction partner, and male versus female partners. Each of these scenes is presented with a narrative description of the situation, followed by a prompt from the therapist and a signal for the subject to respond. The client's response is then coded on scales related to social skill as described in Tables 4.1 and 4.2. To ensure that the scenes are relevant to the patient, we employ the name of a real person the patient might interact with. To aid the client in paying attention to the description of the scene, we ask him or her t. read the description using "I" statements. Sample role plays and one patient's responses follow.

Scene 1
P: My car is in the shop for repairs. Karen offers me a ride to and from work while the car is getting fixed. I am very pleased with her offer. She says
A: I know you won't have a car for a few days. I'll be glad to pick you up and bring you home in the evening.
P: Ah. Ah, well, I'll see if I can make other arrangements first.
A: OK. I know I had a problem getting around the last time my car was in the garage.
P: Well, if I need to I'll let you know.

Scene 2
P: I'm watching my favorite TV program with Karen. She unexpectedly changes the channel to another TV show. The show I was watching was almost over and I want to see the end of it. I'm annoyed. She says
A: Let's watch this channel for a while.
P: Well, wait a second, I want to see the rest of that show.
A: You know you've been watching *your* shows all day. This one's better anyway.
P: Let's just see the end.

Scene 3
   P: I'm out to dinner with my family and Joey is going to order a sandwich for me,
      but I'd rather have something else. He says
   P: You are going to have that sandwich, aren't you?
   P: I'd really like a salad.
   A: But, if you order something else, you'll miss the special on the sandwich.
   P: Then I'll pay for it.

Scene 4
   P: I've had a day at home and have been working hard cleaning the house. Bill
      comes home and says
   A: The house really looks great.
   P: Well, it should. I spent all day cleaning it.
   A: Yeah, it looks like you've been busy all day.
   P: I have.

A unique aspect of our role-play assessment is the inclusion of two
additional scenarios that are individually designed for each patient, based on
information gleaned from the clinical interviews. Often these scenes are
samples from the negative-assertion performance class, but, on occasion,
scenes from the positive-assertion class are included. These are scenarios that
are particularly distressing for the patient and are usually exemplars of poor
performance employed by the client to support a conclusion of low personal
value and increased depression. Here is an example of a personalized role
play.

   P: I'm feeling sad at work. A coworker notices and says
   A: Don't be so sad.
   P: (long pause) I don't want to say anything.
   A: All you have to do is smile. Why aren't you smiling?
   P: I have nothing to smile at.

Chiauzzi, Heimberg, Becker, and Gansler (1985) found that such scenarios
produce behavioral differences and are seen as more relevant and realistic.
Clients in personalized, as compared with standard, scenes spoke more
softly, took longer to respond, spoke longer, and had fewer speech
disturbances. More component behaviors, such as the number of smiles and
voice tone, correlated with measures of depressed mood from personalized
scenes. These data suggest that personalized scenes are indeed more related to
symptoms of depression.

Extended Role-Play Assessment

These assessments occur during the early phase of treatment and represent
an attempt to recreate the scene as described in the checklist assessment and
to role-play the scene as close to the client's version as possible. In contrast

with short role plays however, these role plays can be of greater length and variety and more tailored to the client. The therapist can persist in refusal for more than two rejoinders, can display anger or joy, or can inject an unexpected response such as refusal to talk about the topic.

The primary purposes of extended role plays are to assess the likelihood of response deterioration in longer interaction and to determine if the client detects social cues and modifies her or his behavior on the basis of these changing cues. Role plays of this nature can show, for example, that the client continually interrupts her or his partner before the partner has a chance to finish a sentence (a problem with floor shifts), or we might find that, in setting the scene, the client has ignored important cues about the other person (a problem of detection of the partner's emotions). We include here an example of an extended role play for the performance class *negative assertion*.

T: Oh, How are you doing today?

C: Good, How are you?

T: I noticed that you went over to the restaurant for lunch today. I thought that you might want to go over there with me sometime.

C: Sure, Oh, sure! (full volume and enthusiastic inflection) (client immediately recognizes this as an entry to dating, and she does not want to date this man at all. Yet she fails to stop this situation from unfolding, despite adequate recognition.)

T: That really makes me happy. I've been watching you and thought that maybe we could go out on a date sometime.

C: Well, I don't know. Let me see. I've been seeing this one guy pretty steadily.

T: Yeah, are you really serious with him?

C: Um, pretty much, yeah. (less volume and enthusiasm)

T: Well, I've been kind of seeing this girl too, but that doesn't mean that I don't want to go out with you. I think you're somebody special, and I can put someone else aside just to go out with you. (changing the topic away from her boyfriend and the ability to use this as a basis of refusal)

C: Um, Well, I don't know. (spoken very softly and somewhat slurred; failure to redirect back to her boyfriend and the refusal)

T: It's nothing big. We don't have to make a big deal out of it. (continuing to press her because of her display of signs of ambivalence)

C: Well, we'll see. I don't know. (more ambivalence)

T: You mean you don't want to go out with me. (he correctly assesses that the reason for her ambivalence is her desire not to hurt his feelings. Therefore, he casts her refusal in clear guilt-inducing terms)

C: Um, (nervous giggle). I didn't really say that. (voice pitch rises, and she smiles. This behavior confirms his conjecture that she can be made to feel guilty. She fails to recognize the guilt-inducing strategy and fails to respond to it.)

T: I'm just trying to be nice. I just want to take you out to a nice place. Don't you like people who treat you nicely? (further use of guilt inducing statements)

C: Sure, (loudly and forcefully and once again confirming his conjecture)

T: Maybe go out for dinner and some dancing. You like to do those things. I heard you tell the other girls that you went out to dinner and dancing. (subtle use of guilt here. You obviously go out with other men. Then why not me?)

C: Yeah, I did. (fails again to note the guilt strategy and fails to respond to it)
T: So, how about if we go out this weekend?
C: Well, I can't this weekend. I'm all booked up. (ambivalence)
T: You're all booked up?
C: Yes.
T: How about Sunday night?
C: Um, well, Sunday is a bad day, (spoken softly and hesitantly) I've got to go to work on Monday. (once again showing him that refusals are hard for her)
T: How about next Friday?
C: Um, um. (long pause) Well, maybe. (ambivalence)
T: That's a really good time for me too! I think we should go then.
C: Well. (long pause) My number is in the book. If you want to give me a call, then I'll let you know. (partial agreement and more ambivalence)

This extended role play has demonstrated many problems the client needs to address. She has failed to recognize several important topic changes, failed to recognize the guilt strategy, and failed to recognize that her own ambivalent behavior contributes to the man's persistence. Her voice inflection, giggling, eye contact, hesitancy to respond, and inability to make a direct refusal statement are all problematic. In trying to make her refusal, she has done poorly in both the verbal and nonverbal realms. These verbal and nonverbal displays have been detected by her partner and have been molded by him into a successful strategy to maneuver her into complying with his request.

After the role play, the therapist asked the client to describe how realistic she thought it was. She reported that the emotional feelings experienced in this role play were the same as those she experienced outside the consulting room. She felt disappointed in her behavior, depressed in mood, angry at this man, and hopelessly trapped again. She felt that the role play was a very good reflection of how she behaved and how she felt in this type of situation.

Self-Monitoring

In lieu of direct observation of the patient's behavior by a trained observer, many behavioral researchers and clinicians have required the patient or subject to gather his or her own data. The most commonly used data-collection strategy has been some kind of event log that the patient fills out on a daily basis. Kazdin (1974) and Nelson (1977) reported the advantages and disadvantages of self-monitoring. More reliable and valid data are produced from self-monitoring, as compared with other self-report methods, yet these data are still subject to distortion and inaccuracy. Self-monitoring can be used for more accurate counting of discrete events such as the number of phone calls made to friends during the week. Self-monitoring can be biased because the client is unaware of habitual behavior, or unable to detect the desired behavior, or unable to recall or record the event.

We have our patients keep logs of discrete events as they occur. Initially we employ logs to assess the response consequences for social behavior; to examine the frequency of negative assertion, positive assertion, and conversation; and to gather details about situational variables. Two examples of homework sheets employed early in treatment are provided in Table 4.6.

Table 4.6
Homework Log Sheet

Instructions. Your task on this log is to count the number of times you have a conversation with a friend of either sex. A conversation is a talk with a person where you exchange some information and maybe ask questions of one another. There is not an argument or verbal disagreement. Some positive feelings can be expressed to one another, but usually neither of you asks the other to do something or offers to do something.

Over the next 2 days please record the following information about each conversation you have had. Record one occurrence on one sheet.

date	time	interaction partner (friend, spouse, etc.)	topic(s) of conversation

Setting where conversation occurred: _____

_____

_____

_____

Your impression of your partner's response to you: _____

_____

_____

_____

Homework Log Sheet

Instructions. Your task on this log is to count the number of times you have a disagreement with your spouse, friend, etc. A disagreement consists of your partner's making a request of you that you dislike or wish not to do. You try to express your dislike for this request and try not to carry it out.

Over the next 2 days please record the following information about each disagreement you have had. Record one occurrence on one sheet.

date   time   disagreement partner   topic(s) of disagreement
                      (friend, spouse, etc.)

Setting where disagreement occurred: _____

_____

_____

_____

Your impression of your partner's response to you: _____

_____

_____

_____

Later in treatment, homework sheets are used both as a guide for the new behavior and as an assessment device. Because our concern in this chapter is initial assessment, we will provide examples of these homework sheets in subsequent chapters.

Self-Report

There are eight commonly used assertiveness scales.

1. Wolpe-Lazarus (1966) Assertiveness Schedule
2. Wolpe-Lazarus Assertiveness Schedule Revised (Hersen et al., 1979)
3. Assertion Inventory (Gambrill & Richey, 1975)
4. Adult Self-Expression Scale (Gay, Hollandsworth, & Galassi, 1975)
5. College Self-Expression Scale (Galassi, DeLo, Galassi, & Bastien, 1974)
6. Rathus Assertiveness Schedule (1973)
7. Conflict Resolution Inventory (McFall & Lillesand, 1971)
8. Assertion Questionnaire (Callner & Ross, 1976)

The quality and extent of psychometric data on these scales vary greatly. Three scales have validity data (the Rathus Assertiveness Schedule, the

Conflict Resolution Inventory, and the College Self-Expression Scale). In terms of validity data, the Conflict Resolution Inventory fares best, especially in showing sensitivity to treatment and control conditions. However, it is specifically focused on college students' ability to refuse unreasonable requests and, therefore, might have limited clinical utility. The Rathus Assertiveness Schedule has the most extensive norms, including those based on a sample of 191 psychiatric patients. This patient group, however, did not contain anyone with a depression diagnosis. The College Self-Expression Scale is also specifically focused on college students, and norms exist only for this population. Specific details on the Wolpe-Lazarus scale and other assertiveness scales are reviewed in details by J. G. Beck and Heimberg (1983).

Only the Rathus Assertiveness Schedule and the Wolpe-Lazarus Assertiveness Schedule Revised have been employed with psychiatric patient samples. The Wolpe-Lazarus Assertiveness Schedule appears to have less-than-desirable test–retest reliability (Hersen et al., 1979) and does not appear to be sensitive to treatment effects (Hersen et al., 1979; Hersen, Eisler, Miller, Johnson, & Pinkston, 1973).

Hersen et al. (1979) revised the *Wolpe-Lazarus Assertiveness Scale* to simplify questions and incorporate a yes–no format. We employ this revised scale because it has data available for psychiatric patients. However, it suffers from limited sensitivity to treatment effects. The only other scale employed with psychiatric patients is the Rathus Assertiveness Schedule, which does appear to be treatment sensitive (Blanchard, Turner, Eschette, & Coury, 1977).

SUMMARY

In this section we have briefly presented major issues in the assessment of social skill and proceeded from there to present our model of social skill. Our assessment package consists of a behavioral interview, brief role-play assessments, extended role–play assessments, self-monitoring and self-report, and (self–monitoring) homework assignments. Along with these techniques, we organize the targets of treatment into a hierarchical format and start treatment with the easier targets. Having carried out our assessment in this fashion, we then turn to treatment. Our next section begins with one aspect of treatment, direct behavior training.

Chapter 5
Direct Behavior Training

After completion of assessments, we begin a segment of treatment we call *direct behavior training.* In the first sessions of this segment we concentrate on preparing the client for the more difficult work ahead. We first want to lay the groundwork for this entire kind of treatment. We begin this process by providing a rationale and a description of what will be happening in upcoming sessions. Our rationale for treatment focuses on the client's behavior, the interpersonal nature of social functioning and its effect on mood, and the effects on self-evaluation that follow from less effective social behavior. Here is a typical portion of a session devoted to this topic with our prototypical client. This session took place before the role-play assessment, to prepare the client for the assessment activities and the treatment sessions to follow.

T: I don't know if we discussed this last session, but we have a philosophy that, when people are depressed, it is usually related to some kind of problem with other people and them with you. So it is a whole range of things that might happen when people get depressed. We do not necessarily say that interpersonal problems will cause depression or that depression causes problems with people. But, at least, with the people we have been seeing, we notice that the two seem to go hand in hand. Certainly if someone is depressed and things are going wrong with friends or other people, it makes the depression worse. So, what we try to do is get an idea about why people are depressed; that is why we talk about your feelings and ask you to fill out the questionnaires. We try to get an idea of how you are thinking in social situations and how you react to other people. We can't walk into your house and follow you around, so the next best thing we can do is create an artificial type situation which we call *role playing.* Some of these role plays we use with every client, and some we develop on an individual basis. Then we role-play to see how you respond to those situations. When you get into treatment, the relationships with other people become a central part of what we talk about. We will be meeting for about 5 months, once per week for the first 16 weeks and then every other week for the last month. During that time I will be talking a lot about how you are relating to other people: things you feel uncomfortable about, things you feel insecure about, other people who might be taking advantage of you, how to get things to work out better with other people, getting to feel better about yourself and not so isolated.

We really try to focus on how you are behaving, rather than just talking about how inadequate you feel. We find that when people feel inadequate, they present themselves in that way and this style can interfere with building good relationships. So, we focus a lot on behavior, ways to get your behavior to change. We do a lot of role playing. The typical session will go like this. First, we'll talk about difficult situations, and I'll send you home with homework to write down those situations on a sheet like this (shows homework log). Tell me what the situation is, who was there, what you did, and what you thought and felt. These will tell me what you typically do, who the people in your life are, and how much of what behavior is happening. We will use these homework sheets to develop our role plays. What I find is that I can get a pretty good idea from this homework about the kinds of people and situations you are running into. Then I can see how you do with these situations, and I can show you other ways of handling them. We'll role-play them until you get pretty good at it and comfortable trying these new things. It's like playing tennis. You learn a skill, practice quite a bit, and then go and play a real partner.

We really take the point of view that we are working with you, not doing something to you. We try to work together with you to get this depression out of here. We will explore ways of doing that with you. It is really a problem-solving approach rather than saying something is wrong with you. People have problems and we try to help them solve them. I've said quite a lot. Is this all making sense to you?

C: Every word. It's the most I've gotten out of anything we've done so far. It does address what I'm after, but while you were talking I was thinking to myself "What am I doing here?" Then I think about the office and the trouble I have there. I just can't seem to assert myself and I can't get things done. The same thing happens to me with social groups. So what I do is knock myself down. This is so tiring for me I don't know what to do! This seems like such a difficult problem and so much work.

ROLE PLAYING

Teaching the "as if" Aspect of Role Playing

We think that several important guidelines should be followed in regard to the teaching that surrounds this portion of skills training. Each role-play performance should be set up according to the following checklist:

1. Give the client specific instructions about what he or she should try to do.
2. Demonstrate the desired performance to the client and follow this demonstration with questions, to make certain that the client has attended to the aspects of the performance that are being trained.
3. Ask the client to carry out the role play he or she just witnessed.

4. Provide positive feedback to the client about good aspects of the performance and give new instructions and demonstrations for areas that need to be improved.

5. Give praise for following instructions and trying to carry out the role play and encouragement to continue with the next role play.

The first role plays are usually most difficult for the client, and we have taken a number of steps to ease the client into role-playing techniques. We use the following guidelines in selecting the first role-play scene:

1. Select a situation that is low on the client-created hierarchy. Clients often wish to start with the most pressing problem first. This is usually unwise because highly emotionally charged areas impede new learning and increase the likelihood of poor treatment outcome.

2. Choose an initial response that is not too complicated and can serve to illustrate problem areas in the client's performance.

3. Choose an area that is still relevant to the client.

4. Pick an area where the client can eventually try the new skills in the natural environment.

Following these guidelines, the client is first given instructions about the "as if" nature of the role play. The client should behave as if the therapist really is the close friend and as if this were really happening right now. Next, the specific content of the role play is given to the client. Once this information is conveyed, the therapist should provide examples of good and poor role plays. For example, the therapist would set up an example of a good role play in the following way. The situation chosen for the role play is deliberately bland, in accord with our guidelines of training for easier situations first.

> T: I'm going to show you how a good role play should go. I'm going to pretend I'm on the phone with my friend, Fred. He and I are having a friendly conversation. OK, I'm starting the role play now.
> T: (holding the phone to his ear) Hi, Fred. How are you today? . . . I promised to call you today and I'm keeping the promise . . . Me? . . I am fine . . . I am really glad to talk to you today. You were telling me about your brother last time we talked. Any more news? . . . Really? . . . Yeah . . Uh Huh . . . Well, that's nice . . . Do you really think he'll go through with it this time? . . . Yeah . . . I hope so, too! . . . She seems like just the woman for him . . . I don't understand what he's waiting for . . . Really . . . I think so, too . . Are you going to call me tomorrow? . . . Around seven will be fine . . . Call me at home . . . Good talking to you Fred . . . I'll speak to you tomorrow.
> T: (to the client) You see that I tried to make this as real as I could. I spoke just as if

Fred were really on the phone. I didn't tell you what I would have said, I actually said it. That's what we mean by the as if nature of the role play. When we do a role play together, you would act the part of Fred in this example and speak to me just as Fred would do. Got the idea?

C: I think so.

T: Good. Why don't you try it now, and I'll observe and try to help improve your performance. Ready?

C: OK. (holding the phone to his ear) Hi, Fred. I would say, How are you today? I promised to call him today and I'm keeping the promise. I am really glad to talk to him today. He was telling me about his brother last time we talked. Oh, Oh. I think I did it wrong. I'm not being as if. (recovering) Fred. Any more news? . . . Really! . . . Yeah . . . Uh Huh . . . Well, that's nice. Do you really think he'll go through with it this time? . . . Yeah, I hope so, too! I don't understand what he's waiting for . . . Really, I think so, too. Are you going to call me tomorrow? . . . Around seven will be fine. Call me at home. Good talking to you, Fred. I'll speak to you tomorrow.

T: That was pretty good. You really got into the role in the second half of the role play. You noticed that you were not in role after the first few lines and corrected yourself very well. Many people have trouble getting into role just as you did. You really tried to do it the way I did in the last part, and that is what we're trying to teach you here. Now that you have the idea, let's try some role plays that are based on what you do.

We usually videotape or audiotape all role plays, to avoid depending on memory for what did or did not happen, and we always save all tapes until treatment is ended. These old tapes have often been wonderful illustrations of how much progress a client has made. But, in the short run, the most recent role play can be replayed, and pertinent aspects of the performance can be studied.

A Typical Role-Play Session

Choosing the first role play to train is a somewhat delicate matter. In addition to the picking of a situation that can be a good training experience, as previously outlined, several other factors should be considered.

1. Carry out the first role play as the client usually does it.
2. Focus on situational and molecular aspects of the performance first and train more complicated portions later.
3. After the demonstration of the new performance, ask the client if she or he has noticed the targets chosen for improvement.
4. Train one or two components at one time; for example, voice volume and inflection.
5. Once those components have improved, move on to the next group of two; for example, eye contact and verbal content.
6. Expect performance to deteriorate briefly after the addition of new components.

Our first role play is done according to how the client usually handles the given situation. The client sets the situation and describes how the interaction partner will respond. Once these details have been handled, the first role play commences, with the client acting the role of himself or herself and the therapist following the instructions of the client. Our prototypical client's first role play concerned an episode in which she and a girlfriend were at a local bar, sharing a drink and some private conversation.

C: I am in the bar at the corner with my girlfriend, and this man comes by and bumps me. Then we start talking as I described to you.
T: Okay, I'll be the man and you role-play yourself. Ready. (role playing) Oops. I'm sorry. I didn't mean to bump you.
C: That's OK. No problem.
T: How about if I buy a drink for you and your friend.
C: OK.
T: Are just the two of you here?
C: Yeah. How about you?
T: I'm here with a couple of my buddies. Would you like to dance?
C: No, I think I'll stay here at the bar. I just danced, and I'm a little tired.
T: Well, maybe later.
C: Yeah, that will be OK.
T: (returning later) Are you going to dance with me now?
C: OK.
T: (after the dance). Boy, that was fun, wasn't it?
C: Yeah.
T: Want to go again?
C: No. Why don't we just talk for a while. Where are your buddies?
T: They're right over there. (pointing)
C: So, do you live around here?
T: No. I'm from crosstown.
C: Where about?
T: Over by those condos.
C: Where do you work?
T: At that meat packing plant nearby.
C: What do you do there?
T: I'm a truck driver.
C: Do you live alone? Are you married?
T: I share the condo with my buddy. Gee, I've forgotten how late it is. I've got to go! Bye.
C: Bye.

Within this role play the therapist noticed several problems requiring attention.

1. The client spoke softly, at a barely audible level.
2. The client's voice quality was not lively and lacked enthusiasm.

3. The client generally looked at the role-play partner with furtive glances rather than a more fixed gaze.
4. The verbal content of the conversation contained primarily questions to the partner that gave him little information about the client, leaving him in the position of being less able to extend or maintain the conversation.
5. The conversation moved quickly from a casual one to a more intimate one when the client asked about the partner's living arrangements. He responded to this by stopping the conversation.

The therapist chose to focus on two aspects of the performance first and to ignore the others until later in training. Instructions were provided about what new aspects of the performance were desired, and then a demonstration was given. In this case the therapist acted as follows:

T: I noticed several things about your behavior in this role play. You spoke softly, at a barely audible level, and your voice lacked liveliness and enthusiasm. You occasionally glanced at me while you were talking, but by and large you looked away from me. When you spoke to me, you usually asked questions and gave me little to go on to extend the conversation. Toward the end of the conversation you shifted the topic from a casual one to a more personal one without much preparation. Let's try to improve your skills here. I'd like to start with parts that will be easier for you to learn and to then move to more difficult parts later. Let's start with your voice. People find it easier to listen to you if you speak at a comfortable level and your voice sounds pleasant and lively. I'd like to carry out this role play again except that I'll be you and you be the man in the bar. I'm going to speak louder than you did and try to put liveliness in my voice. While you're pretending to be the man in the bar, I want you to pay attention to my voice. We'll tape-record this too so we can listen to it later and compare it with your original role play. Ready. You start.

The next role play focused on a demonstration by the therapist of the same verbal content, but with increased voice volume and inflection. Because these two types of behaviors do not easily lend themselves to written description, we have forgone a role-play narrative. The therapist did carry out the role play, emphasizing the two voice qualities targeted for treatment. We pick up on the role play where the therapist is inquiring about what the client noticed in the demonstration.

T: Let's stop now. What did you hear in my voice that was different from yours?
C: You were louder than I was all the time, and it was easy to hear you. Your voice seemed more alive than mine, and I felt like you were really interested in talking to me.
T: Good. You noticed both of those important changes. I added liveliness by stressing the last syllable such as ÔK! or by extending that last syllable. When I asked a question, I raised the tone of my voice at the end of the question. When I was disappointed, I lowered the tone and loudness of my voice. Now, I want

you to get a picture in your mind of how I sounded, and I want you to try to sound like I just did. Let's role play again. I'll be the man in the bar and you be you.

Several role plays were than carried out, with the therapist pointing out the improved loudness and greater liveliness of the client's voice. Feedback after the second role play was as follows:

T: This was a really good try! . . . It was much easier to hear you! . . .I also noticed that your voice was more lively. You did emphasize the last syllable to stress a word, and your questions were better too. I think you're getting the idea. You're doing just what I showed you. Let's try it once more, and this time I'd like you to speak even more loudly and with more and stronger emphasis.

Once the client was able to carry out two or three good-quality role plays with improved loudness and tone, the therapist moved on to train verbal content. In this case, training proceeded as follows:

T: You're doing very well. Let's move on to a new area. When you are talking to someone, it's easier on you if you can just ask questions and leave most of the work of carrying the conversation to the other person. Sometimes the other person feels that she or he is being interrogated when you do this. Let's try to give the other person somewhat more to go on, to keep the conversation going. So when you ask a question, you can also give the person some information about you that is relevant to the topic you are talking about. Let's try a role play, and I'll show you what I mean. Remember, pay attention to how I add extra *topic relevant* information.
C: Ready. Oops. I'm sorry. I didn't mean to bump you.
T: That's OK. No problem.
C: How about if I buy a drink for you and your friend.
T: OK! That's nice of you. I'd enjoy a whiskey sour.
C: Are just the two of you here?
T: Yeah. I don't like to come here alone. How about you?
C: I'm here with a couple of my buddies. Would you like to dance?
T: No, I think I'll stay here at the bar. I just danced, and I'm a little tired.
C: Well, maybe later.
T: Yeah, that will be OK. I like slow dances. I don't enjoy the fast ones.
C: (returning later) Are you going to dance with me now?
T: OK! I'm glad you came back.
C: (after dancing) Boy, that was fun, wasn't it?
T: Yeah. It sure was.
C: Want to go again?
T: No. Why don't we just talk for a while. Where are your buddies?
C: They're right over there. (pointing)
T: So do you live around here?
C: No. I'm from crosstown.

T: I've been over there. There are a lot of nice homes there. I enjoy pleasant areas
   like that. Where do you live?
C: Over by those condos.
T: Those condos are new and pretty. I like the way they're designed. Where do
   you work?
C: At that meat packing plant nearby.
T: That's the one that makes those sausages that are so good. It looks like a good
   place to work. What do you do there?
C: I'm a truck driver.
T: I enjoy driving, but I don't think I'd like to drive a truck. You really like it,
   though. Do you live alone?
C: I share the condo with my buddy. Gee, I've forgotten how late it is. I've got to
   go! Bye.
T: Bye. (out of role) Let's stop now. Tell me what you heard and what I said
   differently than you did.

The client noticed the longer, on-topic performance of the therapist. Once
again, several role plays by the client, imitating the demonstration, were
carried out, and response-specific positive feedback was provided by the
therapist. The therapist again pointed out and praised performance that
approximated the demonstrated new behaviors of improved topic-relevant
statements. Several repetitions of these new components were carried out
until the client was able to perform more smoothly and quickly.

Most clients can accomplish about this much training in a 1-hour session.
Sessions like this are followed by practice homework assignments. We send
the audiotaped role plays home with the client and ask him or her to listen to
his or her own role plays at least twice before the next treatment session. At
the beginning of the next session we review the homework. If the client's
performance has not eroded during the week, we move on to the next targets
for training. If erosion has occurred, we backtrack and retrain.

Once we have addressed all of the molecular components targeted for
treatment in this situation, we can move to a similar situation and examine
these components once again. In this case we moved to conversations but
changed to a female partner. We found that our client quickly used several
newly taught behaviors including voice volume, eye contact, verbal content,
and facial expression (smiling).

After several additional sessions focused on the other molecular
components, we felt confident that we had established the basics of a good-
quality response and were prepared to move on to the next level of training;
specifically, we wanted to begin what we call *flexibility training*.

FLEXIBILITY TRAINING

This portion of direct behavior training is aimed at carrying out the
following:

1. "Overtrain" the improved performance by role-playing many repetitions.
2. Aid in the transfer of new skills to other situations by varying the situational context.
3. Set the stage for social perception training by training the client to be aware of dynamic variables.
4. Continue to work within the same response class; in this case, conversational skill.

Training in this area begins by varying as many of the situational variables as possible, one or two at a time. Conversations are role-played with friends in a variety of settings such as while exercising, riding in a car, or talking over the telephone. The therapist continues to provide response-specific feedback, praise, and encouragement. Homework assignments during this phase start out with a diary containing:

1. Situations where conversations now occur.
2. Persons with whom these conversations occur.
3. The topics of conversation.

These diaries can reveal difficulties in any of these areas. There might not be enough availability in any of these areas. There might not be enough availability of conversation partners, there might be too few settings for conversations, or the client's fund of topics to talk about might be too small. Of course, this last area is quite tricky for depressed clients. They usually artificially restrict their fund of topics by editing the conversation severely with the "Is this really an important topic?" axe. Many clients conclude that what they have to say is mundane at best and quite invaluable at worst. They then restrict the topics of conversation to only a few "important matters." For our readers, we address this issue under self-evaluation training, but for our clients we address it in treatment when the problem is evident.

Difficulties revealed by homework in any of the three areas previously listed then become legitimate targets for incorporation into the role-play flexibility training. For example, if the client seems to have too few topic areas in her or his repertoire, homework can be assigned to read or learn about a new topic and come prepared to practice conversations with a friend using this topic. If too few settings are available to the client, then homework could focus on logging all of the client's activities, to see if some settings are being overlooked. Or a homework assignment could consist of observing the conversational behavior of others to see if these people have conversations in settings the client did not think about or had ruled out. Once again, as these settings are discovered, they can be role-played.

Table 5.1
Homework Log Sheet

Instructions. Your task on this assignment is to identify the topic changes that your partner has made as you spoke with her or him. A topic change happens when your partner has been talking about one thing that has a similar theme and then changes to something else with a different theme. Examples are talking about houses and then talking about cars; talking about where she or he lives and then talking about where she or he works.

Over the next 2 days, please record the following information about changes in conversation topics.

---

date	time of day	first topic	second topic	conversation partner

---

The final portion of flexibility training is the beginning of training in dealing with dynamic variables and social perception. This phase consists of homework assignments aimed at gathering information about this class of variables. We begin by asking the client to observe the conversational behavior of interpersonal partners. A typical homework sheet is shown in Table 5.1.

We ask patients to gather observational information about floor shifts, topic changes, and, later, their ideas of the emotional states of their interaction partners. The data gathered from these homework sheets serve as part of the data for the training in dynamic factors involved in social interaction.

SUMMARY:
FLOW OF A TYPICAL DIRECT
BEHAVIOR TRAINING SESSION

1. Ten minutes to review previous homework and incorporate his data into the day's session.
2. Forty minutes to pick particular situations for role plays and carry out the following sequence:
a. The therapist provides information about the components of the new performance being taught.
b. The therapist demonstrates the new performance in a *reverse* role play, in which therapist plays the client and the client plays the other partner.
c. The therapist checks to see that the client has attended to the relevant aspects of the demonstrated performance and understands what is expected of him or her.

d. The client role-plays, with the intent of imitating the demonstration just provided by the therapist.

e. The therapist provides response-specific praise and feedback to the client and encourages the client to try some more role plays. The therapist provides praise for following instructions.

f. They complete several repetitions of the role plays, until the client appears to have improved to at least a minimally adequate level.

g. The therapist trains the client in similar situations or a different set of component behaviors.

3. Ten minutes to assign and explain the homework assignment and set the next meeting time.

At the conclusion of this segment of social skills training, the therapist should prepare the client for the upcoming segment of *practice and generalization*. We now turn to this part of social skills training.

Chapter 6
Practice and Generalization

By this stage, the client has had several opportunities to role-play the new skills we have explained and demonstrated to him or her. As the client becomes proficient in role plays in the office, the next step is to have him or her attempt to carry out the new skill in an actual real-life situation. The term *practice and generalization* refers to the practice of a new skill outside the consultation room but under the guidance of the therapist. We use several procedures to aid this process and make the transition easier and more successful for the client.

1. A performance is not considered for practice and generalization training until the client has completed direct behavior training and attained at least a minimally proficient response.
2. A performance is not considered for practice and generalization training unless homework sheets suggest that there is ample opportunity to try the new performance.
3. The therapist provides instructions about situational, dynamic, and natural reinforcement and punishment factors, to make the practice easier and more likely to succeed. Ideally this guidance should include a written, specific homework sheet, so the client can continually refer to it.
4. The homework assignment is worked out between the therapist and the client before it is assigned.
5. Instructions to the client about the homework should be detailed and specific, and the therapist should insure that the client understands what is expected of him or her.
6. Completed homework is reviewed at the next treatment session, usually via a role play, and the therapist assesses the client's ability to carry out the performance at the minimal level of proficiency or better.

7. If the homework assignment has not met the minimal criteria set out above, then the therapist should retrain that performance.

A TYPICAL HOMEWORK ASSIGNMENT

Homework assignments are particularly important because they constitute "real" application of the newly learned skill. Also the real situation will be more fearsome than the role play and the client is more likely to have his or her new performance disrupted. To combat these difficulties, homework should follow on the heels of direct behavior training. An example of the last role play in direct behavior training for our prototypical client follows. In this example we have moved to the performance class of negative assertion involving the refusal of a request for a date.

T: Let's try this refusal again. Remember you have certain experiences that you can bring to bear on this situation. You know that if you agree to a second date that he will start getting some ideas that this is more serious than you would prefer and you don't want those ideas to occur. So, this is what you want to say and you know that you must stick with your refusal. This doesn't directly say "I don't like you." It doesn't give him the idea that there is something wrong with him. But this is not a good match and not something you want to continue. It doesn't really attack his worth as a person. Are you ready? (Beginning the role play) Hi, would you like to go out again this weekend?

C: Oh. No thank you.

T: What's the matter? We had a *really* good time last week end. I certainly had a good time!

C: I had a very nice time. I told you that I had an excellent time! It was very nice.

T: So, what's the problem, you know? Don't you want to have a good time again?

C: Oh! (loudly and enthusiastically) Of course I do, but I find from my experiences in dating more than once, that sometimes the person gets the wrong impression.

T: Oh. I won't have the wrong impression. We're just friends!

C: No! Maybe that's not like that this time, but I'm going to go with my feelings and experience and stay with the one date and that's all!

T: Gee! I guess you don't like me? Is there something wrong with me?

C: No. I didn't say that! I like you and I think you're very nice, but it's just a rule that I have for myself based on experience that if I date the same person more than once he gets the wrong impression.

T: Yeah! But rules are made to be broken! Everybody breaks rules. Why can't you break this one?

C: No! This is one rule I don't break because feelings just get hurt.

T: Oh, my feelings won't get hurt.

C: There's really nothing more I can say. I don't break this rule!

T: (throws up his arms) Boy! I give up! (out of role now) That was much better! That was really good! That's a really tough situation for you, and you did very well. You said it in a nice way and stuck to your point. You may have bruised

his feelings a little, but you didn't demolish them. People will remember that
you handled it in a very nice way and weren't mean or put them down. Do you
think we can give this a try this week with the fellow who keeps calling you for
a date?

C: Gee, I don't know.

T: Remember to play this in your head before you say it, and you'll have a good
success there!

C: Yeah.

T: So could you try it with him? Let me give you this homework sheet that
describes what you're supposed to do so that it is like our role plays. This
fellow is one you really don't want to date any more but have not been able to
say "no" to, so you leave the phone off the hook. He doesn't seem to get hurt
easily, so it should be easier with him. It will be easier for you if you make your
refusal as soon as he asks and not be vague like you were before and have him
call back three or four times. You know he usually calls on Tuesday or
Wednesday, so I want you to rehearse the role play in your mind on those days
and have your homework sheet by the phone. Turn on the tape recorder so I
can hear what you have said and be sure to bring the tape in with you, and we'll
review how you did. Here's the homework sheet. Is all that clear? (Note that
the tape recording is of *one-half* of the phone conversation only, just the
client's portion.)

C: Very, but this is going to be hard.

T: You've done very well with it here, so you just do what we have role-played.
OK?

C: All right.

At this point the therapist gave the client the homework sheet shown in
Table 6.1 for this assignment.

Table 6.1
Homework Sheet: Trying a Refusal

Instructions. You are going to try to refuse a request for a date made to you over the telephone.
You should post this sheet by the phone, in case you need to refresh your memory. On the days
when this type of phone call is most likely to happen, read through this sheet and rehearse your
response in your mind. These are the points you should remember and make in your refusal.

1. You have had this kind of experience before.
2. If you agree to another date, this man will think that the relationship is becoming more
   serious.
3. You say NO to his date request and stick to it, saying NO repeatedly if necessary.
4. Don't say "I don't like you."
5. Don't say there is something wrong with him.
6. Say that this is not a good match and that you don't want it to continue.
7. Don't attack his worth as a person.
8. If he persists in his requests, repeat your NO and add that there is nothing else you can say.
9. Say good-bye.
10. Try to keep your voice volume up.
11. Do not say "maybe," "I'll think about it," "I don't know," "I'm booked," or "I've got a
    boyfriend."

Tape-record your part of the conversation and bring it with you for our next session, and we'll
review it together.

T: Read through this sheet now and see if this is clear to you.
C: OK.
T: Any questions?
C: You really want me to practice this in my head?
T: Yes. It will help you stay on track and remember what you want to say, and it
will keep you from drifting off the topic of refusing. Any other questions?
C: What if he doesn't call on Tuesday or Wednesday?
T: Rehearse it each day anyway, just in case he calls. If he doesn't call, then we'll
try it next week or with someone else. Any other questions?
C: No.

REVIEW OF A HOMEWORK ASSIGNMENT

This client was also experiencing difficulty with providing praise,
encouragement, and attention to her child. During direct behavior training,
several role plays were carried out to improve her skill. Her usual tendency
with the child was to not recognize good behavior. She rarely gave
unsolicited attention to the child or spent time with him when he was being
good. Role plays focused on approaching the child when he was being good
and giving him a brief hug, following this with conversation about whatever
he was doing. The first homework assignment followed from these role
plays. The client was to approach the child not less than twice or more than
five times in the evening, hug him, and then proceed to talk with him for at
least 5 minutes. The homework sheet is shown in Table 6.2.

Table 6.2
Homework Sheet: Giving Positive Attention to Your Son

Instructions. You are going to give your son a brief hug and talk to him about what he is doing.
You should approach him without his invitation and first give him a hug, and then talk about
what he is doing. Only approach him this way when he is behaving according to the expectations
you have already given him. Make sure you ask him questions about what he's doing and ask
him if it's fun. Do not do things for him or give him advice about how to do it. If you can assist
him by providing something, then you can do that without his request. For example, turn on the
light for him, or put the pieces on a flat solid surface. Talk with him about what he is trying to do
and how he's trying to do it. After about five minutes say good bye to him and let him continue to
play.

1. Do these things at least twice and not more than five times each evening for the next 7 days.
2. Tape record at least two of these on two different days, for a total of four recordings.
3. Continue to do this even if he does not respond positively at first.
4. Be sure to be physically close to your son. Do not talk to him from across the room.
5. Do not talk to him while you're doing something else. He should have your undivided
attention.
6. Stay on topics related to what he is doing or wants to do.

Review of this homework session began as follows. *J* was the clients' son.

T: Hi, How are you?
C: Fine.
T: Did you try the homework assignment?
C: Yes, I did. It seemed to go hard at first, but it got easier the more I did it. I brought the tape.
T: Let's listen to the first one (playing the tape)

(From the tape)
C: Joey, that looks like fun. What do you want it to look like?
J: Like the picture here.
C: You really like that one, huh? It sure looks complicated, and you're sure working hard at it. Is it fun?
J: Yup, but I can't get this to stay.
C: Here try putting it on this. It will stay better. What do you do next?
J: This, I think. And then this.
C: That looks right to me. I'm going to watch you try it.
J: Sure, Ma. My friend at school has one like this, and he did it all by himself.
C: You're doing it by yourself, too! It's such a good job you've done so far. How long did it take your friend?
J: A couple of weeks, but I'm doing pretty good so far.
C: You sure are. That seems to work better over there. I'm going to go now, but I'll stop by later to see how good this looks. Bye.
J: Bye, Ma.
(Therapist stops the tape)

T: You did very well with this one. Did you hug him when you first started?
C: Yes, and he was fine with that.
T: Good. You stayed on the topic of his building and gave him some assistance, but not advice. You told him that you would see him later and then said goodbye. You gave him your undivided attention while you were talking to him. It sounds like you did this very well. The only thing I can see that could be improved is to stay with him somewhat longer before you leave. You followed the directions very well. Shall we listen to another?

The other taped homework assignments showed equally good performance, and the therapist concluded that the client could carry out a competent homework assignment for this performance. The therapist then turned to a secondary issue in this assignment, how the boy responded.

T: How did your son like the "new you?"
C: He's better. I don't have to holler at him so much, and he seems happier. It makes me feel good too when I don't have to be nasty to him. I feel better about myself as a mother.

PROBLEMS WITH HOMEWORK
ASSIGNMENTS

An analysis of poorly administered homework assignments can highlight a number of instructive issues. In the next example the therapist makes a number of mistakes. These begin with the last role play of direct behavior training, in which .the client has not yet acquired a minimally proficient response. Homework is assigned anyway, and the assignment lacks a number of the specific parameters that should be present such as specific instruction for the client, guidelines about when, where, and with whom to try the new skill. Little is given to the client to assist in carrying out this shaky new skill, and no systematic manner of monitoring the actual performance is suggested. We begin our example with the last role play of direct behavior training.

T: Hi! I was wondering if you would like to go out to the movies with me this weekend?
C: Oh. Oh, I don't think so. Thank you.
T: But. (long pause) Are you doing anything?
C: Ah, ah, ah, this weekend? Yes I am.
T: Oh, but next weekend you're free, right? (loudly and forcefully)
C: Well. Well, next weekend I could think about going, but I'm really not interested in going. (very softly)
T: How come? (softly and with a hint of sadness)
C: Well, um, ah . . .
T: (interrupting) I thought we were friends. (softly and with sadness)
C: We are friends! (loudly, with increased pitch, light and happy) That's all. We're just friends. That's all. (loudness drops off)
T: So don't friends go to the movies?
C: Well, I suppose they do sometimes. I'm just not interested in dating at this time.
T: This isn't a date! It's just a get-together.
C: (giggles and smiles) Oh, all right, I'll go. (loudly, light, happy) But we're just friends. Just friends!
T: (out of role) Oops. You shouldn't do that. What the heck does "just friends" mean. You did well up to this point. You need to stick to your position and say that I know we're just friends, and friends can go to the movies together. But, I have the feeling that this will not work, and I prefer not to go.
C: Write that down for me. I have a date this Saturday that I have to get out of. Oh, my God (loudly and with a giggle), I'll never remember this!
T: Just remember to say no and that you have had this happen before and you have the same feeling about this now. Then just say I have this feeling and I prefer not to go. Clear?
C: I don't know.
T: You'll do fine. Try it this week. If you want to, try it for this Saturday night's date. OK?
C: I'll try.

HOMEWORK LATER IN TRAINING

As the client progresses in ability to carry out a proficient response in both the office and the guided homework, the therapist should move toward less structure and direction in homework assignments. Homework sheets should become less detailed and gradually phase out all together.

Later in treatment the focus moves away from molecular components and response quality and toward training in the detection of and response to dynamic and situational stimuli. Initial homework during this phase focuses on teaching the client to pay attention to these cues, moving toward using them as a signal to change an ongoing performance. We will discuss these types of homework assignments in the next chapter.

Chapter 7

Social Perception and the Dynamics of Social Behavior

Throughout this book we have stressed the idea that social interaction is a fluid communication process. What is now being said and done is affected by what has been said and done in the past and by what is expected in the future. Up to this point we have focused our training on the more easily defined aspects of social skill such as voice volume, inflection and posture. In this chapter we tackle the more difficult, yet critically important, part of social behavior, that is, the dynamic aspect. In our endeavour here, we have, unfortunately, less research to go on. Only recently have systematic inquiries into the flow of human interaction been undertaken (for example, by Faraone & Hurtig, 1985).

During training in social perception skills and the dynamics of social behavior we try to have the client:

1. Recognize the various dynamic cues as they are presented.
2. Understand social norms.
3. Imagine and carry out several responses to these dynamic cues.
4. Monitor her or his own dynamic cues and modify them to improve communication.

Our attempt to achieve these goals is based on a series of procedures we employ in each of the eight areas of dynamic stimuli listed in Table 4.3. Here are the training procedures we use:

1. Provide information to the client about the particular dynamic cues targeted for training.

59

2. Demonstrate these cues and variations of them, teaching the client to recognize them in others' behavior.
3. Supply information on how the client can respond to these cues.
4. Demonstrate potential responses to these cues.
5. Provide opportunities to practice recognizing these cues in others' behavior and responding to them.
6. Rely on various aids to training including flash cards and videotaped feedback, because many of these cues are subtle and difficult to explain and demonstrate.
7. Carry out repeated practice until the client appears to have minimally mastered recognition and response.
8. Move on to the next target for training or to practice and generalization.

We now turn to examples of training in several target areas that are common for our clients, which have been drawn from several clients working on different target areas.

TARGET AREAS: USING FLOOR SHIFTS AND TOPIC CHANGES

We have found that these two problems often occur together, so we usually teach them simultaneously.

Floor shifts are signals from the speaker to the listener that indicate that he or she is about to terminate the message and yield the floor to the listener. A variety of verbal and nonverbal cues can signal a floor shift, including decreasing the loudness of one's voices at the end of a sentence or phrase, asking a question, making direct eye contact, and gesturing to the partner that it is now her or his turn. Many floor shifts are signaled by a prolonged pause or by the content of the sentence coming to a logical conclusion. Two primary difficulties arise for clients regarding floor shifts, and they are interruptions and silences.

Topic changes occur when the conversation shifts from one theme to another. A number of problems can arise in this area.

1. Failure to detect a topic shift by the conversation partner and failure to redirect the conversation back to the original topic.
2. Drifting from one topic to the next and continuing to talk, thereby not allowing the conversation partner sufficient opportunity to speak.
3. Shifting from the original topic to another topic when emotions intensify.
4. Staying on one topic and refusing to shift or coming back to the same topic over and over again.

An aid to training that we have sometimes used with difficult clients is a paper sign labeled *The Floor*. The person may only speak when in possession of this sign and must surrender the "floor" when not speaking. Another is labelled *"Off Topic"* and is utilized to signal clients when they are drifting away from the focus of conversation. These flash cards make subtle cues more salient. They are employed frequently in early sessions and gradually withdrawn over the course of treatment. Our example comes from a client who had difficulty giving up the floor to the other person and continued to talk on, shifting from topic to topic. In this case the focus of training was to keep the client on topic, to the point, and shifting the floor to the conversation partner. For this client, we used both feedback cards, The Floor and the Off Topic cards. This role play occurred during flexibility training.

T: Let's try this role play again. I'll be the employee, and you act your usual role as the supervisor. When I hear you drifting off topic, I'll flash this card at you and you should come back to the main topic. You hold the floor card and pass it to me when you are done talking. If I have something I wish to say and you have talked too long, I'll ask you for the floor. Then you must hand me the card and listen while I talk. Ready? You start.

C: (role-playing) I asked you in here today to talk about your absences from work. This is the second time we have talked about this, and it is quite a problem. We depend on you to handle the payroll and cannot function when you are gone so much. In the past you told me about your family and how ill they were. These things can be hard. We talked about . . .

T: (flashes the off topic card)

C: But, you know that. Five days in the last four weeks you did not come to work, and you did not call to say you weren't coming. We didn't know if you were coming or not. I don't like to do these things, but I have to. You remember the trouble we were having with John. I didn't . . .

T: (flashes the off topic card)

C: Oh. For you, I am going to put you on probation for the next 3 months to see if this can be improved. You will have to try to be more reliable like Frank. He is a good model. I never have to . . .

T: May I have the floor please (reaches for the floor card)? You're right about these 5 days. I have been very concerned about my mother, who is very ill, and I forgot about everything else. I apologize for not calling, and I realize that I have caused a good deal of upset here. I just wasn't thinking. Could you consider a 1-month probation rather than 3 given these circumstances? (gives the floor back to the client)

C: Why didn't you say so in the first place. I think 1 month is a reasonable time period. But I want to make sure you act more responsibly! Is that point clear? (gives the floor to the therapist)

During these role plays we wanted the client to realize that he was drifting off topic and that the listener noticed this and began to look frustrated. The Floor and Off Topic cards served initially as highly salient cues but were gradually phased out, so that the client came to depend more on the change in demeanor of the role-play partner. During this training, we employed videotaped feedback of the role play, focusing the client's attention on the facial expressions of the interaction partner whenever the client began to digress. Beyond the goal of recognition of a digression as it occurred, we hoped that the client would more quickly recognize off-topic thoughts and edit them out of the conversation before they ever appeared for the role-play partner to react to.

TARGET AREA: CLARIFYING THE OTHERS' COMMUNICATIONS

Accurate communication requires that the listener receive the intended message. There are occasions when messages become distorted because they were not stated clearly, because some issue was missed, or because nonverbal behavior modified the meaning of the verbal message. Problems in this area are rectified by training the client to summarize what has been received and to feed this summary back to the interaction partner and request that the summary be verified as accurate. This skill requires the client to pay attention to the communication from the interaction partner in order to later give an accurate summary. Consequently, we usually start by focusing on paying attention to the other person, which includes the following:

1. Stop any other client activity (reading, eating, daydreaming, watching TV, and so on).
2. Arrange for little or no distraction by moving out of noisy areas, congested areas, and so forth.
3. Keep floor shifts and topic shifts to a minimum.
4. Display behavior that indicates that a message has been received, to keep the flow of information coming (head nods, yes, uh huh, and so on).
5. Take the floor to stop further information flow when a reasonable amount of information has been received.
6. Feed back what has been received and ask for verification.

An example of this training revolves around conversation with a client's mother. In this role play we again used a flash card and video feedback as aids to training. Our flash card said *Summarize and Verify*. These two tasks were a necessary step in preparing the client to voice disagreement with his mother's point of view. But first we needed to train accurate reception of information. The role play went as follows:

C: Gee, Ma, I just took out a loan to get my car painted. But I found out that my car is pretty old and that it would not be economically wise to use this money for that purpose, so I put the money in the bank. I wouldn't dare put this money into the car.

T: But you got this loan anyway.

C: Yeah, but I put it right into the bank.

T: Now this is a perfect opportunity to start saving for a house. Take this money and put it away. You didn't have it before. No big deal. So that's OK. But all your other bills fall due at once, car insurance, this other loan that you have. You have to start paying on a school loan that you have. You've been out of school 2 years now and finally called them and told them that you want to start paying back on this loan. So they said "wow, you're way behind. You owe a lot of money in back interest. And we want that money right away." So now you're really down. (flashes the Summarize and Verify card)

C: Boy Ma, you sure said a lot. Let me see if I understand you. You think I should start saving for a house, but you're worried about all my other bills, and you think I'm going to get depressed again. Is that right?

T: Yes that's right! You put this money away, but I don't know if you can let it sit there and struggle away with your paycheck. I know you. You want to be able to pay everything you have to pay. So, I was worried that you would get down right away. Oh, boy, I don't want that to happen.

C: Thanks Ma. I know you're worried about me and I'm glad you're concerned. I think I can manage this all right, and I do want to start saving for a house.

T: (out of role) You did a fine job of summarizing what your mother has said to you and then feeding that information back to her. You found out that she is worried about the financial stresses you might be under and she is worried that you might get depressed again. Once you are clear about her concerns, you can then form a better response, which you did. You acknowledged her concerns and told her that, in general you are glad that she is concerned about you. But, in this specific case, you have things under control. Did you see where she was rambling on about all the things she was worried about? That's where you need to interrupt and clarify before you get sidetracked. Let's look at the videotape and see where the rambling started. Then let's try this again.

This initial role play demonstrated a good response, but the identification of when to make the response was determined entirely by the therapist. The video replays were used to point out the other's behavior, which should serve as a cue for the client to make his very able response. Several repetitions of this scene were carried out, gradually reducing the use of the flash-card prompt. Once this skill had been mastered, other similar scenes were trained, so that the client would easily recognize when to summarize and verify his mother's communications.

TARGET AREA: RECOGNIZING AMBIVALENCE AND BEING PERSISTENT

The goal of this training is to increase the client's proficiency in recognizing verbal and nonverbal cues that indicate ambivalence on the part of the listener. The verbal cues we expect clients to recognize are statements by the interaction partner such as

1. I'll think about it.
2. Maybe, well, sort of.
3. I'll decide (or do it) later.
4. I'm not sure.
5. Not yet, not ready yet.

Nonverbal cues include

1. A long period of silence after a request has been made.
2. A change in voice volume or pitch with a yes or no response.
3. Facial expressions indicating that the other person is thinking or uncertain about his or her answer or statement (avoidance of eye contact, pursing of lips, and staring at the ceiling, and so on).
4. Gestures indicating uncertainty (rubbing one's chin, scratching one's head, and so forth).

In the following role play our male client is calling his friend to set up a time to play tennis. His friend is usually hard to pin down to a time because of his ambivalent response. In this role play, the therapist used a flash card with *Ambivalent* on it to aid the client in identifying this type of response. In direct behavior training, the client had already been trained to make a specific request. The task at hand was to recognize the ambivalent statement and follow it with a direct request.

T: Let's try this phone call with your friend. You call him and set a time for a tennis match. I'll be your friend and respond as he does. When I make an ambivalent response, I'll show you this card to help you recognize it. When you see the card, then you should make a direct request for a meeting time. OK, ready? You start.
C: (hand to his ear as if on the phone) Jim, hi. How are you?
T: Good! I'm glad you called. What's on your mind?
C: Well, I'd like to plan a tennis match with you at the club. Are you interested?
T: I guess I am. (flashes Ambivalent card)
C: Are you sure you want to play this week?
T: Yes.
C: Thursday evening from 6 to 7 would be good for me. How's that for you?
T: I don't know. I might have to work late, but I'll try to be there. (flashes Ambivalent card)
C: You're not sure. How about Wednesday at the same time? Can you give me a yes or no for that time?
T: Maybe. Shirley might come over for dinner. I'm not sure. (flashes Ambivalent card)
C: Can you give me a yes or no for Thursday?
T: Well, OK yes. (now out of role) That was good. Each time I was vague, you

responded with a specific request. Because this is a phone conversation, you can only go on what I say. Let's replay the audiotape and listen to what I say. See if you can identify the hallmarks of ambivalence we talked about earlier. After that, let's try the role play again, but I won't use the flash cards.

In situations where the client might ordinarily have access to nonverbal information, training relies more heavily on video feedback. After a role play has been completed, the video is replayed, and the client is asked to pay attention to the nonverbal aspects of ambivalence first and then to the verbal aspects.

TARGET AREA: DETECTING THE OTHER'S EMOTIONAL STATE

Detection of another's emotional state is a very difficult task. Yet the emotional tone of the other person can be an important clue in predicting interpersonal outcomes. Our clients are most often concerned with identifying and avoiding unpleasant emotional states such as anger. We spend a good deal of time teaching them to detect and respond to these states. It is also important for our clients to be able to detect positive emotional states. Even though our clients often report being less concerned with this issue, we feel that equal emphasis is warranted.

Clients are taught to recognize verbal and nonverbal components of behavior that are usually indicative of a positive state. We identify the following components:

Verbal cues
1. "I" statements indicating happiness – "I feel good." "I'm happy."
2. Statements indirectly indicating happiness — "Things are going well." "What a wonderful day."
3. Indirect statements from others indicating happiness – "He's in a good mood today."
Nonverbal cues
1. Smiles from the other person.
2. Singing, whistling, clowning, joking.
3. Mode of dress (for example, bright or pleasant colors).
4. Speech rate that is normal or slightly fast.
5. Usual things done with a flair and requiring extra expenditure of energy (for example, tossing a hat onto the coat rack).

Negative emotional states include sadness, anger, and irritation. Cues for these states are divided into verbal and nonverbal cues also.

Verbal cues

1. "I" statements expressing annoyance or anger.
2. Indirect statements indicating emotional tone – "What a lousy day."
3. Indirect statements from others indicating emotional state.
4. Verbal silence.

Nonverbal cues

1. Increased or increasing voice volume.
2. Increased or increasing pitch.
3. Increased or increasing speech rate.
4. Increased use of sharp, quick gestures.
5. Disrespect for property, exemplified by throwing things, slamming doors, pounding walls, and so on.
6. Change in eye contact to a fixed stare directly into the partner's eyes.
7. Widened eyes, flushed face, tense muscles in face, jaw.
8. Rapid changes in body position.
9. Abrupt floor changes (interruptions) and or topic changes.

In general, we presume that intense emotional states preclude rational behavior, and, therefore, we also include under this category any other state that impairs a person's ability to process information. Such states can be produced by alcohol, drug use, fatigue, or illness. When the interaction partner's cognitive abilities are impaired, we recommend to our clients that they discontinue the interaction and suggest that conversation resume at some later time when full cognitive ability has returned. Of course, there might be times when such a course is not prudent, such as with a sick child who must take medicine.

One client, a middle-aged married man, had particular difficulty detecting the positive and negative emotional states of his spouse. He would often approach his mate when she was tired and irritable and present her with a litany of complaints associated with his depression. Her usual reponse to this behavior was increasing annoyance, punctuated by terse statements that he should go seek some help. Previous homework assignments had detected this pattern, and role plays were now focused on the client's skill in detecting his wife's degree of irritability. Earlier, in direct behavior training, his conversational skill had been addressed, as had his style of making complaints. Flash cards were employed at first to display the emotional state being depicted, and role plays were videotaped and replayed so that the client could study nonverbal cues. He was taught to pay attention to his wife's indirect verbal cues and to the nonverbal cues indicating slowed production of behavior. A role play focused on the indirect verbal cues went as follows:

> T: (as the client's wife) Hi, I'm finally home. (sighing) What a terrible day. (displays flash card *Annoyed and Tired*)

C: I'm not feeling too chipper today, either. I'm down in the dumps.

T: Don't add to my day.

C: Oh boy. Give me those things (taking her case) while I tell you about the good things that happened today.

T: OK, that sounds fine. (out of role) Let's stop here and watch the video to see what non-verbal cues you can pick up to aid you in figuring out my mood. Concentrate on the behaviors we discussed before. You did a nice job of detecting my mood after the flash card and of switching the topic. That's an important skill, and you did it well. You need to pick up on her mood as quickly as you can and tailor your behavior to fit. Let's look at the tape now.

Homework assignments with another client revealed that she and her husband would bring up difficult topics in the evening after her husband had been drinking. Homework revealed that these discussions quickly became very unpleasant arguments and failed to resolve any problems. She was schooled in evaluation of her husband's sobriety. She was taught to look for slips of speech, ruddy complexion, motor coordination problems, and the smell of alcohol. Detection of any sign of alcohol use was to be employed as a clear signal to postpone serious discussion until her husband was entirely sober. She role-played scenes in which he had started a difficult discussion and she had detected alcohol and then postponed the conversation. She also role-played scenes in which she had started a discussion and then detected signs of alcohol use. An example of one of these role plays follows:

T: I'm going to be your husband just returning from his friend's house. You should bring up the topic of a vacation. You know he does not want to go because of the expense. If you see any of the signs we've talked about, you should immediately postpone the conversation, tell your husband why you've stopped, and switch topics or stop talking. Ready? Keep an eye on me. (starting the role play) Hi, I'm back.

C: Hello, Jack. Come sit down by me. I've been wanting to talk to you about that trip to Hawaii.

T: Oh, not that again.

C: Shelly called this morning and gave us some great news. All of the kids chipped in together and bought us a tour package to Hawaii.

T: Really. (slipping in the chair and knocking a pencil off the table) We (pause) still (pause) need to pay for the rest?

C: I think we had better stop talking about this now. You've been drinking. Let's talk about it in the morning when you're fresh. What did you do at Alex's?

T: We're planning on a fishing trip this Saturday. (out of role) That was very good. As soon as you saw unusual behavior you reacted immediately and pointed out your husband's state and switched the topic. That was done quite well.

A final example involves a man in his 30s who continues to have difficulty with his mother. She continues to strongly suggest that he should or should not do something and then quickly becomes angry when he disagrees with her. Previous homework had gathered information about the frequency of such encounters. The goal of training during this series of role plays was for the client to recognize the very first occurrences of his mother's behavior, which inevitably led to later anger. As soon as the beginning of this sequence was detected, the client was taught to immediately change the topic. Role plays with this focus proceeded as follows:

T: Let's try another role play. I'll be your mother again. Remember the cues you are looking for. She always begins by asking you what you have done about your clothing, your job, or your car. As soon as you hear that in my role play you should immediately change the topic. Is that clear? Ready? I'll dial the phone and call you. (starting the role play) Hi, Bruce. I've been dying to talk to you today. How are you?

C: Good, Ma. I'm glad you called. It's been so very busy at work, I haven't had time to turn around. My assistant has been out sick for the last 2 weeks, and I've had to do his job and mine. I'm really exhausted.

T: I'm so proud of you, Bruce. You always were a hard worker. And I know you always do an excellent job. Your father and I were just talking about what a hard worker you are. Your father said that you probably haven't asked for a pay raise yet (displaying flash card *Change the Topic*).

C: (interrupting) Mom, Mom, just a minute. I wanted to talk about Dad some more. I've been concerned about how he's feeling. Do you think he'll want to go to the ball game this Saturday?

T: Yeah, he's feeling better. He's not here right now. He said he'd like to go and was kind of looking forward to it. (out of role) That was very good. You immediately interrupted your mother when she began to talk about your job and what you should be doing there. Then you followed up with a compelling topic change. Let's try this again, this time without the flash card.

Repeated role plays of this kind produced immediate recognition of the mother's behavior and immediate shift of topic. Homework was assigned to observe her behavior and shift the topic in their next telephone contact. Review of homework revealed partial success. The topic shifting had worked briefly, but the mother had returned forcefully to the neglected topic. The client felt that this return to the topic was inevitable and would always lead to a nonproductive argument. At this point the therapist introduced the concept of *minimally effective response* (Rimm & Masters, 1974). A minimally effective response refers to the client's behavior and is characterized by gradually increasing the strength of application of a new behavior until the desired outcome is achieved. In this particular case, the therapist considered the following increases in the strength of the shifting-topic behavior:

1. Tell the mother that he does not wish to speak about this area and switch the topic.

2. Each time the mother switches the topic back, recognize the switch and shift off the topic.

3. Each time the mother shifts back to the topic, detect it and respond with a statement that he does not have time to talk now, but must go. He then says good-bye and that he'll call later. Subsequent calls must be at least 8 hours later.

Discussion of these alternatives resulted in the choice of number 3, primarily because 1 and 2 were estimated as likely to not be effective. Role-play training continued, with two goals. As soon as the mother suggested one of the difficult topic areas, the client was to switch topics, as previously learned. If the mother brought up the same topic again, the client was to interrupt and use the pressed-for-time response to terminate the phone call. A typical role play went as follows:

> T: Let's try this again. You have to detect the beginning of one of the difficult topics and change the topic and then stay alert for the first attempt to bring this topic up again. As soon as you see that the same topic is returning again, you should say that you're in a hurry and will have to go. Remember to say that you'll call again later. Ready? Let's try it. (therapist in role) Hi, Bruce. I've been dying to talk to you. How are you?
>
> C: Good, Ma. I'm just so busy with work, you know. My assistant has been out sick for 2 weeks and I've had to do his job and mine. It's really been tough.
>
> T: You've always been such a hard worker. Your father and I are so proud of you. We were just talking about you yesterday. Your father was wondering if you'd asked for a pay raise yet.
>
> C: (interrupting) Ma, Ma, just a minute. I wanted to talk about Dad some more. How's he been feeling lately? Do you think he'll be interested in going to the ball game this Saturday?
>
> T: He's feeling better and he's been talking about the ball game. He's not here right now, but I think he'll want to go with you.
>
> C: I'm glad he's feeling better. I was worried about him. I know he loves to watch baseball. Besides, I like seeing him. I guess I'll come by about the same time Saturday to pick him up. Remind him to bring his hat, will you?
>
> T: All right, Bruce. I'm sure he'll be glad to go. But you know we both are worried about your job and your salary. We were . . .
>
> C: Mom, Mom, don't worry about my job. I'm 34 years old and I'm able to make my . . . oops. It's getting late and I've got to go. I'll call you later. Good-bye. (pretends to hang up the phone)
>
> T: That was a very good job. You detected the changes in topic very quickly, and the first shift of topic went very well. You sure picked up the shift back to the job topic quickly, and you did say you had to go and end the conversation. When you first detected a return to the job topic you started to respond as you usually do and then caught yourself. You know that this response always leads to an argument. Let's try this again, and try to catch yourself sooner and stop that old response before you start it.

Many more role plays were carried out until the client felt able to actually carry out this response with his mother. At that point this task was assigned as homework, and the client was instructed to tape-record his half of the phone conversation and bring the tape into the next session. Review of the tape showed a good-quality response, and the client reported a successful outcome.

TARGET AREA: REINFORCING OR PUNISHING

Interaction partners often have the ability to control resources and information that aid or hinder a client. The partner might choose or not choose to deliver these resources to the client. During training the therapist tries to tie three concepts together for the client. These concepts are the norms of positive and negative reciprocity, the other's emotional state, and the actual provision of reinforcements or punishments. Clients are taught that the other person's emotional state can be a strong clue about whether she or he might actually provide reinforcement or punishment. Reinforcements include such commodities as the other's time or abilities, and the use of or provision of a physical entity (a car, money, advice). Punishments can be failure to provide such commodities as expected or removal of previously provided resources (I want my lawn mower back. You're fired). Clients believe that positive emotional states, such as being happy, are indicators that the person is more likely to provide positive reinforcement, and negative emotional states are more likely to yield punishments.

Positive reciprocity means that a person is likely to return a positive reinforcement after having received one. Negative reciprocity is an analogous concept applied to punishment. Applications of reinforcements or punishments are likely to also effect the other's emotions, thereby adding to the positive or negative reciprocity effect. Work in the area of marital discord has shown that relationships that are not satisfying are characterized by a high display of nonverbal behavior indicating social punishment and also high rates and immediate return of punishments following a tit-for-tat mentality (Birchler, Weiss, & Vincent, 1975; Vincent, Friedman, Nugent, & Messerly, 1979).

Positive reciprocity follows a similar time course, with couples tending toward highly correlated rates of production of reinforcers over a 24-hour period (Wills, Weiss, & Patterson, 1974). Satisfied couples were able to extend the time frame of their exchange ledgers for both reinforcement and punishment so that accounts might not balance at the end of a day but would balance in the longer run (Gottman et al., 1976). Tying these various concepts and studies together for social-perception training yields the following notions:

1. Requests for favors are best attempted when the other person is in a good mood.
2. Provision of punishments to others is likely to result in negative reciprocity.
3. Provision of reinforcements to others is likely to lead to positive reciprocity.
4. Offers of reinforcements to others that are not solicited and that do not require immediate repayment are likely to move a relationship toward more intimacy.
5. Provision of punishments in intimate relationships can cause them to deteriorate.
6. Friendships and romantic relationships require the development of trust, which is based on a reinforcement and punishment history and a balance in the long-run approach.

One final goal that does not derive directly from the research on couple satisfaction but that we have included in our goals is a verbal–behavioral correspondence. The goal is for the client to behave in a manner consistent with what has been said.

For example, one client had particular difficulty with negative reciprocity. One of the role plays with this client is presented next. This client complained of loneliness, social isolation, lack of interest in others, and anhedonia in social interaction. Conversational skill was chosen as one target for treatment. Direct behavior training had taught the client to increase the use of social reinforcers such as "I'm glad you came by today," "It's good to see you," " Nice talking to you," and "You're always welcome here. Come again." These new skills were having a positive effect but were being inhibited by the client's tendency to employ negative reciprocity. If the conversation partner did not show up one day, this client would retaliate by not being available for the next usual meeting time. Worse yet, this client would occasionally refuse to talk to his partner and would simply remain silent. He felt that his behavior was a suitable response to the poor treatment he had received from his partner. His role play proceeded as follows:

> T: Last week Fred didn't stop by for your usual coffee break and talk. You said that he did come by the next day, and you just didn't talk to him. Remember what we talked about with the norm of negative reciprocity. If you punish someone, he or she is likely to punish you back quite quickly. You in turn will want to return the punishment. A relationship can be seriously harmed by such a negative reciprocity spiral. Let's see if we can break this spiral before it even starts. I'll be Fred in this role play, and I'll be coming in for our usual coffee break get-together. I didn't show up yesterday and never told you I wasn't coming. Your task in this role play is to use all of the positive conversational

skill you've learned before, but you must also avoid punishing your friend. Instead, you express your disappointment at not seeing Fred and ask that he let you know if he cannot come as expected. Ready? Let's try it. (moving into role) Hi, Rob. Is the coffee ready? I hope there are some good rolls today.

C: Hi, Fred. Good to see you today. I sure enjoy our talks. By the way I missed you yesterday. I wish you'd have let me know you weren't going to be here.

T: I get busy you know and forget. My boss was hovering around so much, I forgot about you. I'll try to call.

C: Ya darn well better! Oops. Try to remember will ya! So what's happening with your vacation plan?

T: Let's stop here. You did very well for the first try. You were positive and told him how much you enjoy your meetings, and you mentioned your disappointment. You also asked him to change his behavior. Then you slipped into your more punishing style for a minute and then caught yourself. Let's try this again. See if you can stop the punishing style before it even slips out this time.

One final example comes from a lady who was having difficulty with her fiancé. She complained that he had treated her poorly several times while they were out shopping. At the time of occurrence she had said nothing to him. Later that evening she decided to confront him with the issues and get them settled there and then. She marched over to his apartment and let herself in. She found him in the shower. She entered the bathroom and accused him of treating her badly that afternoon. He responded by asking her to leave the bathroom. She then threw his clothes into the shower with him and proceeded to throw in his pillows and linens. After this she left. He responded to this treatment by leaving town for a few days without notifying her of his whereabouts. Role plays focused on the norm of negative reciprocity. Information about the likelihood of a return of punishment was explained. Further, the client was told about the *bank account model*, in which couples did not immediately return reinforcements or punishments. An alternate course of action was suggested, as outlined.

1. She had legimate complaints about poor treatment.

2. She was more likely to have her prospective mate understand and modify his behavior if she presented her complaints tactfully and at the right time.

3. He would be more likely to be upset because she was telling him personal and private information, and she could improve her chances of getting her message across if she chose a private time when they could be alone and not distracted.

4. She had strong positive feelings for this man regardless of this current event, so she should first remind him of her strong feelings and her commitment to him. She could add to the strength of this display by being physically close and by giving affection.

5. She could bring up the *specific* events of that day and relate how they made her feel. She would follow this with a request for new behavior from him.

Repeated role plays with these components were carried out until the client had reliably achieved a good response. Homework was assigned to carry out this new series of behaviors when the next mistreatment occurred.

SUMMARY

This chapter has presented several targets for training involving the dynamics of social behavior. These skill areas are more complex than those included in direct behavior training and are more difficult for the client to acquire. In addition, the conceptual aspects of this training can conflict with the client's beliefs and attitudes about his or her own performance and other's behavior. Social skills training would not be complete if these cognitions remained unaddressed. The next chapter describes training focused on cognition.

Chapter 8

Self-Evaluation and Self-Reinforcement

As noted in chapter 2, substantial evidence exists that depressed individuals tend to make inappropriately negative self-evaluations and to sparsely self-reinforce. Depressed clients might overlook important positive information and focus almost entirely on the negative. Objectively successful behavior can be seen by depressed clients as failure, resulting in the application of self-punishment rather than self-reinforcement. Such cognitive activity by clients can seriously interfere with therapeutic efforts, and it therefore requires that active steps be employed to minimize its impact.

Soon after the beginning of direct behavior training, the client is introduced to self-evaluation and self-reinforcement procedures. These procedures are entirely intertwined with direct behavior training and social perception training. There are four goals the therapist hopes to accomplish with these procedures.

1. Improve the client's ability to attend to important details and not overlook critical information.
2. Help the client base self-evaluations on the technical adequacy of her or his behavior rather than on others' responses to it.
3. Help the client develop more rational and lenient standards for self-evaluation.
4. Increase the range of positive self-reinforcers the client can use and increase the rate of application of these reinforcers.

CHANGING THE CLIENT'S FOCUS

During direct behavior training and social perception training, the therapist focuses the client's attention on aspects of his or her own and other people's behavior that are often overlooked. Refocusing of the client's attention happens during the information and the feedback stages of direct behavior and social perception training. As the therapist primes the client for an upcoming role play, she or he often provides information about what the client should be attuned to and what the client should do. During demonstration role plays, the therapist might point out specific behaviors to which the client should attend. Several replays of the video- or audiotaped demonstration can be employed to highlight salient aspects of the new skills about to be tried by the client. Subsequent to such a display, the therapist can ask the client to close his or her eyes and imagine carrying out this new performance, paying particular attention to the specific behavioral components pointed out during the information and demonstration procedures.

After a role play has been carried out, the therapist once again can influence the client's propensity to focus attention on certain aspects of her or his performance. Almost all of our training sessions are either videotaped or audiotaped, and in fact, both modalities are often used. The therapist can now play and replay the role play, stopping and starting, to point out a certain behavior that is important to the client. The therapist can inquire about whether the client noticed a particular behavior or not and suggest that he or she pay attention to this behavior in the next repetition. Before the next role play commences, the therapist might have the client list the various components she or he should be attuned to. The clinician's office can be equipped with a chalkboard or an easel with newsprint to allow a listing of particular aspects that are important for improved role-play performance. Once listed, this information can serve as a ready aid to the client struggling to learn new skills.

An example of this process is taken from the early stages of direct behavior training with a client experiencing difficulty with expressing annoyance when mistreated and with refusing requests. This client had loaned a substantial sum of money to this girlfriend, and, when he requested repayment, she would respond by accusing him of being cheap and of endangering the relationship with his petty behavior. He would characteristically agree with her assessment of him and stop pursuing the issue. Initial training focused on the verbal content of his message and the ability to persist with this content.

> T: Let's try to handle this role play differently this time. I'll play you, and you play your girlfriend. I want you to watch me and then for you to later do and say what I just did. I'm going to try to be more persistent with my request for more money back. I'm going to make a simple request for a return of the money and then just keep repeating the request without changing the tone of my voice. I'm going to try to not get diverted to another topic or to get angry or feel hurt. I just want to stay on track and get my message across. I know this is not the way you do it, so I want you to pay close attention to what I say and do.

When we're done, we'll look at the video of this. Ready? I'll be you at your house when she comes over. (moving into role) Hi. Boy, I'm glad to see you!

C: Aren't you going to let me in?

T: Sure, sure, come on in.

C: I've had a rough week. I'm a little short again.

T: I know, but I'd like to ask you to give me back the money I lent you.

C: Not this again! I've never seen anyone so cheap! If you don't trust me with money, how are we ever going to get along. I just can't stay with someone like that. Let's forget it, for now.

T: Well, I'd like my money back. It was a loan.

C: What! Come on. I hate this. Stop!

T: I'd still like my money back. (out of role) Let's stop now and review the video. I want you to listen to what I said and watch how I behaved. Then you try to list what I did. (replays video) Now, what did you see and hear?

C: It was sure different from what I would do. Let's see. You just kept saying the same thing and didn't change no matter what she did.

T: Yes. That's right. That's the persistence I told you about. What else?

C: Your voice sounded the same. I would have gotten sheepish and quiet. You didn't.

T: Yes. Anything else?

C: I would have told her that I didn't want this relationship to end and that she was scaring me by saying that. You just acted like she hadn't said that. I would have been hurt and mad when she called me cheap. You just seemed to go right on.

T: Yes. Very good. You noticed all the things we talked about. The persistence, the repeating with the same voice tone, and not getting sidetracked. That's what I want you to try with me. Think for a minute about how you might act just like me. Remember what I've just done and see if you can get all the parts into your role play.

SHIFTING THE CLIENT'S
INFORMATION BASE

After training of the client to attend to new and different information about an interpersonal interaction, the stage has been set to change the information base the client employs to support self-evaluation judgments. During the earlier phases of direct behavior training, the therapist has systematically moved the focus of the client's attention toward specific behaviors. As this process continues, the client acquires two data bases upon which to make evaluation judgments. Most clients base their judgments of quality on effectiveness alone. If their behavior accomplished the goal they set out to attain, then, a priori, their performance was of good quality. The therapist's constant focus on social interaction behavior as a skill and on the mastery of various subcomponents of this skill introduces a competing data base unrelated to effectiveness. Having primed the client in this fashion, the therapist introduces the next procedure, which is more forcefully designed to replace the client's original data base and at the same time begin to challenge his or her self-evaluation rating system.

INTRODUCING A NEW SELF-EVALUATION SYSTEM

After the client has become facile in detecting specific components of the skills being learned, the therapist introduces the following grading system, tied to the new data base. Letter grades between *A* and *F* are assigned to an entire performance by the client. The anchor points for these letter grades are derived from the particular components the client is learning.

For example, if the client is attempting to improve eye contact and head movement, then the grading system ranges from *excellent (A)* to *very poor (F)* in gradations of these two behaviors. During the feedback portion of training, the therapist asks the client to assign a letter grade to the performance, based on the restricted skills currently under focus, and the therapist does the same. Often these two grades disagree, with the therapist's grade exceeding the client's grade. Should this occur, the therapist should proceed to examine the basis for the disagreement. The client is usually asked to explain her or his criteria for each rating point on the scale, and then the therapist does the same. Absolute, perfectionistic standards are commonly employed by clients. Faced with this situation, the therapist needs to point out the relative nature of his other scaling, which is individually tailored to the current skill level of the client and incremented in steps up from this level. Clients often employ an absolute standard and increment downward to levels still not self-attainable. The therapist should point out that such a system guarantees high rates of low self-evaluation and punishment, even in the face of progress. Additionally, the client might fail to include all of the important components in her or his evaluation and include data that are irrelevant according to the data system set up previously. These errors should be corrected by replay and repetition of the role play, with the therapist pointing out the various important components and their relative ratings. After completion of the evaluation, the next role play should commence.

An example of the use of the grading system involves a client who felt underrecognized at his job. He felt that his supervisor gave all the best assignments to his office mate and not to him but that he was equally qualified. He described himself as quiet, and he had not mentioned any of his concerns to his supervisor. Role plays had been focused on his making a request of his supervisor for some of the work he desired. The focuses of the current role plays were the verbal content of his talk and his voice volume and inflection.

T: I'll be your boss in my office. You knock and come in to discuss the next few jobs coming up, to see if there are ones you'd be interested in. When you see one you like, you volunteer for that one. Remember, first you ask to talk to me about the upcoming work. Then look for one you're interested in and then volunteer. While you're talking to me I want you to imagine that I'm hard of hearing and that you have to shout at me any time you talk to me. Ready? You start.

C: (knocks on desk) May I come in? I wanted to talk to you about the new jobs coming in. I'm interested in whatever new work is coming up.

T: Oh let's see. There's the budget data coming that will need to be analyzed and put in a report to the regional manager. Then the receiveables data is coming soon. New employee lists are due soon and need to be verified with payroll. We're going to need someone to work with PR on the new promotional campaign. That's about it, so far.

C: I'd like to volunteer for the budget project. I'm sure I can do a fine job with it. Can you give that one to me?

T: Well, you haven't done a big one like this. OK, but keep in touch with me as you are doing it.

C: Yes, I will. May I start today?

T: Of course. Is that it?

C: Yes, thank you.

T: (out of role) Let's stop here and replay the tape. Pay attention to what you did and said, to see if you matched my demonstration.

C: OK. Well, I asked to talk to him about new jobs and then, when he listed them, I saw one I liked. Then I volunteered for the job I wanted and asked if I could start now. I told him I could do a good job. My voice was louder all the way through this time. It didn't trail off like it usually does.

T: Do you want to include any other information on which you should base your grade?

C: No, I think that's it.

T: Keeping all those things in your mind, how would you rate your performance on our a to f scale?

C: Oh, C+ seems about right.

T: Why did you give yourself a c+?

C: Oh, I just thought about my office mate and how he might have handled it. I don't think I did as well as he would have. I'm sure he would have been smoother and would have gotten an even better assignment. Besides, I'll bet that the boss will always think of him first.

T: I rated it an A. You did everything you were supposed to and even threw in the request to start now on your own. Your voice was good through the whole thing, and that's a big, big improvement for you. It went smoothly for you, and it all flowed together. I didn't use your office mate's behavior as part of my standard the way you did. Remember, we're trying to keep our focus on *you* and *your* behavior. I just compared your behavior with your earlier role plays and to the skills you're learning now. On that basis, I saw a very fine performance, and assigned the a grade.

C: Yes, but I'm going to have to compete with my office mate and will have to measure up to his standard.

T: What is effective and natural behavior for him might not be for you. We're trying to improve your behavior and tailor it to you. Would you judge how well your clothes fit and look by wearing your office mate's clothes? As you suspect, they aren't your size or style and won't look right on you. So, if you judge your clothes by his size, you lose no matter what. His clothes won't fit you and, your clothes aren't the right size and style. That's the same point I'm trying to make with your behavior. It's unique to you and your style and must be judged by how well you carry it out and by how it fits you.

C: Gee, I hadn't thought about it that way. If I think like that, then I would agree more with your letter grade and would say a $B+$. That's much better, and I feel better about it.

T: You did everything you were supposed to do and a little more and, compared with your earlier behavior, that's a big improvement and deserves a good grade. If you think about it more carefully, you can see the difference, can't you?

C: Yes, uh huh. I see what you mean. I want to try this again.

INCREASING AND BROADENING SELF-REINFORCEMENT

This aspect of training is carried out in conjunction with self-evaluation training, in order to tie self-generated reinforcements to particular self-evaluations. In the early stages of this training, the therapist provides displays of the self-reinforcements he or she attaches to a particular rating. Ordinarily the first occurrence of self-reinforcement happens during the therapist's demonstrations of a performance the client is learning. After the therapist reviews his or her own performance and assigns a letter grade, self-reinforcing statements are made. It is important for the therapist to vary the types of statements employed, to broaden the client's ability to use similar statements. Examples of self-reinforcing statements include:

1. That was quite good. I didn't forget anything and it went smoothly.
2. Much better than last time. I'm getting the idea and getting better all the time.
3. That was easy, and it went so quickly. I felt like I knew what I was doing.

Later in training, the therapist should focus on the client's role plays. During the evaluation phase of feedback, the clinician should provide reinforcement tied to the letter grade evaluations. For example, a client who carried out a technically good response would receive a letter grade of B. Therapist feedback includes focus on specific components, the letter grade, and reinforcement, as follows:

T: That role play was quite good. Your eye contact was very good. You managed to keep your eyes focused in an area around my face and not look at the floor. You leaned toward me the way I showed you, and you didn't put your hands behind your head. I would say that this role play rated a B. You did the whole thing very smoothly and naturally. It was a very fine job, natural, and seemed to be part of you. You're getting better at this. You seemed to work hard at this, and it sure showed.

HOMEWORK: SELF-EVALUATION
AND SELF-REINFORCEMENT

Improper evaluation of homework tasks by the client can also seriously interfere with progress in treatment. To combat such a problem, the therapist should employ similar self-evaluation and self-reinforcement procedures in to homework assignments. Besides specific information about the task to be accomplished and information on when and where to try the new skills, homework assignments should include written instructions for the client to evaluate her or his performance, based on how well she or her performed the various components targeted for improvement. Recall that the natural tendency of most clients is to base their entire evaluation of quality of response on its ultimate effectiveness. To forestall this approach's being instituted with homework tasks, the clinician should stress which data base the client should employ to support an evaluative judgment. Review of homework tasks should follow the same format as review of role-play performance. The therapist should attempt to keep the focus on the skills targeted for treatment and then request a letter grade evaluation from the client. Next, the therapist should review the components he or she perceives and then provide a letter-grade evaluation coupled with self-reinforcing statements. If the two ratings disagree, the therapist should try to move the client's ratings towards the therapist's evaluation by reviewing the targeted aspects of the performance and pointing out behaviors that might have been missed or underplayed. A typical homework sheet with the self-evaluation criteria is displayed in Table 8.1.

Table 8.1
Homework Sheet: Handling Unreasonable Treatment from Your Mother

---

Instructions. During the next week you are going to try to discourage your mother from giving you unwanted advice and insisting that you follow it. These topics come up in phone calls and should be addressed as soon as you detect the beginning of the process. You should not try this yet in face-to-face contact. Your goal is to switch the topic away from these areas and to continue a pleasant conversation about some other topic. If your mother redirects the conversation back to the undesirable topic and continues to give unwanted advice, you should immediately end the phone call. Be polite but forceful in ending the call and remember to promise specific future contact. You should do the following things:

1. Continue the same rate of contact with your mother.
2. Immediately change the topic during phone calls when your mother talks about *your job, your car, or your clothes* and begins to give you advice. Interrupt your mother and move to another topic.
3. *Keep your voice volume up!*
4. Continue to talk about any other area, and, if one of the taboo topics does not come up, politely end the conversation and plan for the next call.
5. If one of the taboo topics is reintroduced by your mother, you should *IMMEDIATELY*

interrupt her and tell her that you're busy and have to go. Quickly schedule another calling time and immediately say good-bye.

6. Do not try to argue with your mother or convince her of your ideas. This has failed repeatedly in the past.

7. Remember that the goal is to make the conversation with your mother more enjoyable and less guilt inducing.

8. Do these things for this entire week in any phone conversation with your mother.

9. Tape-record your half of two of these conversations and bring them to the next session.

10. Evaluate each phone conversation, using the $A - F$ letter-grade scale you have learned. Try to focus only on the skills you are trying to master and to make your judgment on that basis. Record the date of each phone call and letter grade on a 3″ × 5″ card and bring this card with you to the next session.

Chapter 9

Some Problems and Limitations of Social Skills Treatment

As previously indicated, treatment-outcome studies have demonstrated that social skills training procedures are effective and offer the promise of relief from depression for many patients. However, it is not the most appropriate and effective treatment for every depressed client. Some clients are better treated with other types of psychotherapy, and others might benefit most from pharmacotherapy. Unfortunately, research to determine which type of depressed client would most benefit from which type of psychotherapy has not been conducted. We can only offer our speculation about treatment–patient matching, partly supported by our own data. We speculate that clients who:

1. Steadfastly oppose the connection between interpersonal behavior and depression usually do not comply with treatment and are not likely to benefit from it.
2. Do not allow the therapist to control the pace and strategy of treatment are not likely to benefit.
3. Refuse to attempt the homework assignments are not likely to benefit.
4. Have rigid, maladaptive cognitive styles are less likely to benefit.
5. Have interpersonal difficulties in the areas of positive or negative assertion are likely to benefit.
6. Accept the idea that they must do something differently in order to improve are likely to benefit.
7. Have ready access to supportive people in the environment are more likely to benefit.

TYPICAL APPLICATION
PROBLEMS LEADING TO
TREATMENT FAILURE

The heart of this approach is a learning-oriented model. Any factor that interferes with the acquisiton of new skill reduces or destroys the therapeutic effect. The most common problem facing new therapists is *too little practice of new skill*. The new clinician carries out a demonstration, follows this with one or two role plays, and asks the client if he or she is able to carry out the new performance. Overpractice is a much safer error to make for the benefit of the client. Rather than allow the client to decide when she or he is ready, the clinician should observe for improved performance, paying particular attention to shorter latencies to respond and less anxiety about the new skill. As these data begin to come into line, the client can be asked to try out the new skill.

We assume that the strength of a behavior or cognition is directly related to its frequency of use. Frequently used behaviors or cognitions must be consistent with the rest of the person's abilities and must attempt to solve some repetitive problems faced by the client. Viewing behavior from this perspective means that role-play repetitions are not likely to even approach the absolute number of repetitions of the old behavior accumulated over years of use. Hence, overtraining in role plays is hardly likely to be real overtraining in comparison with natural training in the environment.

Therapists faced with clients who have been unable to master a new skill should try to be creative in designing aids to assist in the learning process. Any aid that makes a behavior easier for clients to identify assists in this process. Over the years we have used many such devices for clients and then faded them as the clients begin to master the new skill. Some of these aids are included in Table 9.1.

OTHER PROBLEMS IN TREATMENT

A number of other difficulties have occurred that are related to social skills training treatment. Usually the course of treatment of depression is smooth and causes the clinician little concern. Impediments to treatment can be perplexing for the therapist. The examples presented here could aid the therapist in early recognition and corrective action.

Social skills training, as described here, is an individual psychotherapeutic approach. Inherent in this approach are several procedures that might be the source of difficulty. One problem area has been the therapist's dependence on the client as the sole source of information. Clients could inadvertently (or deliberately) not provide important information to the clinician. The clinician might address a problem in a less-than-adequate fashion when

Table 9.1
Aids to Social Skills Training

Problem	Aid
Client speaks too softly	Have client stand up when talking
	Have client put cotton in ears
	Have client talk over noise
	Have client talk over greater distance
Client drops head and has poor eye contact	Tie bell to hair, movement rings bell
Client looks away at one spot	Place mirror in spot so client sees herself or himself
Client does not use hand gestures	Place objects in client's hand to be given to clinician one at a time
Client uses too many gestures	Place heavy objects in client's hand
Client misses important cues	Use flash cards
Client forgets skill components	Post list behind therapist in client's visual field
Client interrupts	Use *Floor Card*

hampered by inaccurate information. An example of such a state of affairs occurred with a woman depressed over the state of her marriage and her financial affairs. Initial evaluation revealed difficulty with displaying affection toward her husband and difficulty with negative-assertion skill surrounding financial decision making. Delineation of role plays seemed to indicate a highly unresponsive, nonattentive husband. Naturally, one focus of treatment revolved around obtaining the husband's attention by eliminating distractions, choosing the right time for discussion, and other techniques. Second, role plays focused on the client's ability to deliver a clear, unambiguous message. Homework applications, however, continuously failed. After several sessions of treatment, the client revealed her suspicions that her husband was often intoxicated and involved in a sexual relationship with another male. Shortly after this revelation, the husband announced his plan to leave and live with his male lover.

A second problem area has arisen on occasion, once again as a result of the individual focus of treatment. Another woman, depressed over the state of her marriage, responded very favorably to treatment. She became much more self-sufficient, as her husband had desired. She was able to devote energy to her job and was recognized by her employer for her improved performance. She addressed a number of child rearing issues with her husband, and satisfactory solutions were achieved. She reported feeling entirely relieved of her symptoms of depression and able to take command of her life and enjoy it. Her husband echoed her comments and felt she had improved immeasurably. He then announced that he felt this was a very good time to leave the marriage. He had felt that he could not leave earlier because his wife did not appear to be able to function, and he was beset with guilt over leaving her in a semi-helpless position. Over the previous 4 months she had shown such improved ability to manage her life that he felt much less guilty about leaving the marriage. This information came as a complete surprise to the client. The therapist had only met the husband briefly during the initial evaluation and, therefore, had no information about the husband's position in this matter.

A third example involves a young single man who appeared for treatment complaining of depression related to his job situation. He reported several difficulties in both positive and negative assertion with his direct supervisor. He felt that he was very capable of handling his job responsibilities as well as other job functions. Role-play training focused on communication between his supervisor and him, specifically, on disagreeing with his supervisor and suggesting other alternatives. Training also focused on providing recognition to his supervisor when his ideas proved useful. The client learned to apologize when he made an error yet press his point in a new or different situation. His previous behavior had been characterized by withdrawal and moodiness. His supervisor was so impressed that he recommended the client for a promotion, which was quickly granted. The promotion involved the management of a similar operation, but in another city. Such a move proved difficult for the client because of the separation from friends and family and resulted in reccurrence of depressive symptoms and return to the original city.

A number of clients have complained of depression because of the undesirable states of their marriages. In such cases they might face an intractable problem in a marital partner who is unwilling to make any change. One such case involved a women who was quite unhappy and distressed about her marriage. She had been married for about 2 decades yet felt little trust and affection from her husband. He insisted on separate finances for both of them, with a clear splitting of operating costs for their household. The home was divided into his space and her space. Each did his or her own cooking, shopping, and laundry. Vacations were always planned and taken separately. He had several affairs with her full knowledge and she had, in spite, done likewise. Each effort on her part to improve trust, increase sharing, and create intimacy was unceremoniously rebuffed by him. Skills training had attempted to increase positive assertion, positive reciprocity, and interpersonal trust. The client followed directions carefully and performed competently, yet there was no change in her husband's position. In this case, the client's abilities had improved substantially, and her attempts to improve her situation were well carried out. The husband's intractable position allowed little alternative for the client but to turn elsewhere for positive interpersonal interaction. Rather than divorce, this woman chose to improve the ties to her sisters, and this became the focus of treatment, with good results.

Two additional problems can occur. The moods of depressed clients seem to vary. During the early stages of treatment these variations can become more frequent. Clients frequently obtain some temporary relief because they are beginning what they hope will be successful treatment. Three or 4 weeks of improved mood can follow the onset of treatment. After this, clients often become more despondent, because they have not improved as quickly or durably as they had hoped. Therapists can find themselves faced with upset, crying clients. One remedy is to provide some empathy and understanding to quell the episode and then try to move back to regular treatment. Occasionally clients cannot be consoled so quickly, and clinicians might need to devote entire sessions to "patching" the clients' mood. Clinicians must balance the immediate mood or crisis with the longer term goal of improving clients' ability to cope after being equipped with new, more effective skills. Too many detours into crisis management lengthen treatment duration and could reduce treatment effectiveness.

Suicidal ideation, and sometimes intent, often accompany depressed mood. Most potentially dangerous events have occurred early in treatment, with the bulk of these happening before full treatment had begun. During initial evaluations, we explore thoughts about suicide, check for a formulated plan, inquire about any previous attempts, and investigate whether a friend or family member has thought about or made an attempt. The Scale for Suicidal Ideation has been quite useful in clinical evaluation and quantification of risk (A. T. Beck, Kovacs, & Weissman, 1979). Rarely have we had to deal with a situation as a crisis. If we are concerned about a client, we might arrange extra telephone-contact time or brief extra-session contact. Close monitoring and extra contact times have eliminated any crisis situations for ongoing clients.

Two or three clients did evolve to crisis proportions during our first or second contact, before all of our procedures were in place. Once such case involved a young man who contacted the clinic by telephone and announced that he had a loaded revolver and wished us to convey his final messages and listen for the gunshot. He had been drinking heavily and was obviously intoxicated. Standard procedure had been to have the phone numbers of nearby emergency rooms and police stations available. One of us spoke to this man and gradually extracted pertinent location information while the other arranged police and ambulance intervention. Luckily, we managed to convince him to put his weapon aside and agree to open the door for arriving help.

If we become aware of circumstances that could increase suicide risk for a client, we institute close monitoring and extra contact immediately. One example of ours involved a suicidal young woman in treatment. Progress in treatment had significantly reduced her risk of self-harm. One morning, the clinic received notice that a young man had successfully committed suicide. He was not our client, but we knew that he was a good friend of our young woman. We immediately became highly concerned for her safety and instituted close monitoring and added contact. She was very grateful for this concern and action and assured us that it was not necessary, She reacted with further movement away from suicide as a viable alternative.

Chapter 10

Summary and Conclusion

Over the course of the previous nine chapters we have presented much detailed information about how treatment is conducted, but we have not provided the reader with a macro-picture of the course of treatment. We will briefly provide such an overview as a way of concluding our presentation.

A course of treatment for a depressed person usually encompasses 18 individual 1-hour sessions. Sessions are usually spaced 1 week apart but can be doubled to two meetings in 1 week to make up for lost time. Conversely, clients take vacations, become ill, or have other schedule conflicts, forcing postponement of a planned meeting. None of this has given us much cause for concern. We do become concerned, however, when a client misses three consecutive sessions for either planned or unplanned reasons. Such an extended hiatus forces significant repetition of previously covered material in order to refresh new skills that have not been overlearned. Similarly, failure to carry out homework tasks bodes ill for successful treatment outcome within an 18-session time frame. If a client has been unable to maintain a regular schedule, we typically suggest that treatment be extended, to cover the entire curriculum and provide adequate opportunity to practice skills between sessions. If there is repeated difficulty maintaining a regular schedule, then the clinician might wish to rethink the wisdom of this type of treatment.

In the treatment of dysthymic clients, we employ the Beck Depression Inventory as a weekly monitor of mood, and we supplement this with Hamilton and Raskin ratings every third week. Examination of these instruments for about 80 clients suggests a common pattern. Over the course of the first 3 or 4 weeks of treatment, mood scores trend toward a lower level. About the 5th or 6th week, scores return to their pretreatment levels and hold there for several sessions. Around the 11th session, scores begin a sustained drop and continue in this fashion, reaching levels that are no longer clinically significant. Once these scores have descended, they ordinarily rise again but remain low. At the completion of treatment, scores on all mood measures are in the normal range.

At the 5th and 6th week, we have found that both clinicians and clients are worrying that the treatment will not be effective, and both begin to think of alternative courses of therapy. Our data suggest that a decision at this point is premature and that a rethinking of treatment strategy should occur around the 10th session if little progress has been made.

Another procedure we have found helpful has been to include significant family members in the early phases of treatment. During this stage we provide information to the family about the phenomenon of depression and describe the treatment process. At this time we try to answer questions family members might have. If there is significant worsening in a client, we ordinarily inform the family, unless a client forbids us to do so.

SUGGESTIONS FOR NEW THERAPISTS

It should be obvious to the reader by now that this form of psychotherapy is quite different from the more traditional approaches. There are many more techniques to learn, and the treatment is much more highly structured. We have already specified that certain techniques should follow only other techniques. Most therapists who are new to the treatment feel uncomfortable with all of these procedures. Several things can be done to help therapists along in the process of learning social skills training. These suggestions are based on the training we have given to therapists who are just learning.

First, the new clinician should read and probably reread the treatment manual. Next, he or she should arrange for supervision from someone who has had experience treating depressed clients with social skills training. In the absence of a trained supervisor, we suggest that the clinician try to learn our intervention in conjunction with a colleague. It is important to have an objective critic listen to sessions and discuss strategy and client problems, as even the most experienced therapist periodically becomes stymied, frustrated or both.

The clinician should make detailed pre-session plans, using the treatment manual as a guide. These pre-session plans should be carried into sessions, to serve as an outline and guide. Each session should be audiotaped. After the session, the clinician should listen to the audiotape and have the pre-session plan and the treatment manual available to check, to see if correct procedures were followed. If a supervisor is available, then therapy tapes should be reviewed with this person. Subsequent to review of the completed session, the next session should be planned.

Progress toward the next skill targeted for treatment should be geared toward the rate of client improvement. New clinicians tend to move quickly on to the next item before the current topic is correctly addressed. They should try to pace themselves and avoid moving more quickly than the patient can effectively master new behaviors. And, of course, when new therapists encounter difficulty with a procedure, they are likely to fall back on their other therapeutic skills or style. Supervisors are particularly helpful in pointing out such problems.

LOOKING TOWARD THE FUTURE

Interpersonal interactions consist of a complicated series of perceptions, cognitions, emotions, and behaviors. Although our knowledge of this aspect of human behavior has increased greatly in the last 10 years, there is much that we don't know. Increased understanding could come from better methods of assessing social behavior. The methods described in this volume represent the state of the art, yet they are wanting in many respects. A more ideal assessment system would allow a more natural sample of social behavior and, at the same time, give us much more detail about both interaction partners, with a high degree of measurement accuracy. Such a system would allow a real time analysis of the interaction stream, with sophisticated mathematical procedures to illustrate inter-connectedness between the behaviors of both persons. This kind of system implies a time-series analysis of a stream of behavior as it is occurring. No such technology currently exits. There is promise on the horizon that such procedures and equipment could be developed. As more sophisticated and compact computer systems evolve, simpler solutions of this measurement problem could be forthcoming.

To be clinically useful, such an assessment system would require the development of sophisticated software to carry out the sampling of different measures of behavior. These data would then have to be stored and filtered to take out noise and then entered into some system for reduction and analysis. Data collection would be handled via instruments that continuously monitor the targeted aspects of behavior and physiology. At some point, the continuous data from these sensors would be converted to digital data, to allow computer handling. How intrusive this measurement system can be is another problem. Ideally the measurement process should minimally effect the data being gathered. Certainly these sensors should not interfere with behavior because of comfort or awkwardness.

With more accurate assessment available, psychotherapy might be able to move forward. Clearer understanding of situational parameters and response styles should allow pinpoint treatment. Objective data can be readily obtained to document improvement or the lack of it. Clear-cut data could be a more powerful aid to the learning required in the process of therapeutic change. More accurate self-monitoring could improve the impact of homework done during nontherapy time, thereby shortening treatment duration and strengthening treatment outcome. In the area of social perception, such precise measurement could strongly enhance the recognition of social cues.

As is always true in a science, many questions remain. There is much to be done in the future. We have begun to benefit from what has already been accomplished with the advent of more focused and structured therapies and better assessment. Future improvements appear to be intriguing, as well as beneficial. Events could well follow the course outlined above. However, throughout the history of science, the unexpected has proven to be as important as the expected. Many important findings have been serendipitous. There is little reason to believe that in this area it will be any different.

References

Abramson, L. Y., Seligman, M.E.P., & Teasdale, J. D. (1978). Learned helplessness in humans: Critique and reformulation. *Journal of Abnormal Psychology, 87*, 49–74.

American Psychiatric Association. (1980). *Diagnostic and statistical manual of mental disorders* (3rd ed.) Washington, DC: Author.

Bech, P. (1981). Rating scales for affective disorders: Their validity and consistency. *Acta Psychiatrica Scandinavica, 64*, (Suppl. 295), 8–101.

Beck, A. T., Kovacs, M., & Weissman, A. (1979). Assessment of suicidal ideation: The Scale for Suicide Ideation. *Journal of Consulting and Clinical Psychology, 47*, 343–352.

Beck, A. T., Ward, C. H., Mendelson, M., Mock, J., & Erbaugh, J. (1961). An inventory for measuring depression. *Archives of General Psychiatry, 4*, 561–571.

Beck, J. G., & Heimberg, R. G. (1983). Self-report assessment of assertive behavior: A critical analysis. *Behavior Modification, 7*, 451–487.

Becker, R. E., & Heimberg, R. G. (in press). Assessment of social skills. In M. Hersen & A. S. Bellack (Eds), *Behavioral assessment: A practical handbook*. Elmsford, NY: Pergamon Press.

Becker, R. E., & Heimberg, R. G. (1985). Social skills training approaches. In M. Hersen & A. S. Bellack (Eds.), *Handbook of clinical behavior therapy with adults*, (pp. 201–226). New York: Plenum.

Bellack, A. S., Hersen, M., & Himmelhoch, J. M. (1980). Social skills training for depression: A treatment manual. *JSAS Catalog of Selected Documents, 10*, 92, (Ms. No. 2156).

Bellack, A. S., Hersen, M., & Himmelhoch, J. M. (1983). A comparison of social skills training, pharmacotherapy and psychotherapy for depression. *Behaviour Research and Therapy, 21*, 101—107.

Birchler, G. R., Weiss, R. L., & Vincent, J. P. (1975). A multimethod analysis of social reinforcement exchange between maritally distressed and non-distressed spouse and stranger dyads. *Journal of Personality and Social Psychology, 31*, 349–360.

Blanchard, E. B., Turner, J. Eschette, N., & Coury, V. M. Assertiveness training for dental students. *Journal of Dental Education, 1977, 41*, 206—208.

Boswell, P. C., & Murray, E. J. (1981). Depression, schizophrenia, and social attraction. *Journal of Consulting and Clinical Psychology, 49*, 641–647.

Brown, G. W., & Harris, T. (1978). *Social origins of depression: A study of psychiatric disorder in women*. New York: Free Press.

Callner, D. A., & Ross, S. M. The reliability of three measures of assertion in a drug addition population. *Behavior Therapy, 1976, 7*, 659–667.

Chiauzzi, E. J., Heimberg, R. G., Becker, R. E., & Gansler, D. (1985). Personalized versus standard role plays in the assessment of depressed patients' social skill. *Journal of

Psychopathology and Behavioral Assessment, 7, 121–133.

Comstock, G. W., & Helsing, K. J. (1976). Symptoms of depression in two communities. *Psychological Medicine, 6,* 551–563.

Coyne, J. C. (1976a). Depression and the response of others. *Journal of Abnormal Psychology, 85,* 186–193.

Coyne, J. C. (1976b). Toward an interactional description of depression. *Psychiatry, 39,* 28–40.

Coyne, J. C. (1985). Studying depressed persons' interactions with strangers and spouses. *Journal of Abnormal Psychology, 94,* 231–232.

Dean, A., & Ensel, W. M. (1982). Modelling social support, life events, competence, and depression in the context of age, and sex. *Journal of Community Psychology, 10,* 392–408.

Dean, A., & Ensel, W. M. (1983a). The epidemiology of depression in young adults: The centrality of social support. *Journal of Psychiatric Treatment and Evaluation, 5,* 195–207.

Dean, A., & Ensel, W. M. (1983b). Socially structured depression in men and women. In J. R. Greeley (Ed.), *Research in community mental health: Vol. 3.* Greenwich, CT: JAI Press.

Derogatis, L. R., Lipman, R. S., & Covi, L. (1973). SCL-90: An outpatient psychiatric rating scale: Preliminary report. *Psychopharmacology Bulletin, 9,* 18–27.

Doerfler, L. A., & Chaplin, W. F. (1985). Type III error in research on interactional models of depression. *Journal of Abnormal Psychology, 94,* 227–230.

Eisler, R. M., Hersen, M., Miller, P. M., & Blandchard, E. B. (1975). Situational determinants of assertive behavior. *Journal of Consulting and Clinical Psychology, 43,* 330–340.

Endicott, J., & Spitzer, R. (1978). A diagnostic interview: The Schedule for Affective Disorders and Schizophrenia. *Archives of General Psychiatry, 35,* 837–844.

Endicott, J. E., Spitzer, R. L., Fleiss, J. L., & Cohen, J. (1976). The Global Assessment Scale: A procedure for measuring overall severity of psychiatric disturbance. *Archives of General Psychiatry, 33,* 766–771.

Ensel, W. M. (1982). The role of age in the relationship of gender and marital status to depression. *Journal of Nervous and Mental Disease, 170,* 536–543.

Faraone, S. V., & Hurtig, R. R. (1985). An examination of social skill, verbal productivity, and Gottman's model of interaction using observational methods and, sequential analyses. *Behavioral Assessment, 7,* 349–366.

Ferster, C. B. (1965). Classification of behavioral pathology. In L. Krasner & L. P. Ullmann (Eds.), *Research in behavior modification: New developments and implications* (pp. 6–26). New York: Holt, Rinehart and Winston.

Ferster, C. B. (1973). A functional analysis of depression. *American Psychologist, 28,* 857–870.

Ferster, C. B. (1981). A functional analysis of behavior therapy. In L. P. Rehm (Ed.), *Behavior therapy for depression.* New York: Academic Press.

Frank, J. D., Gliedman, L. H., Imber, S. D., Nash, E. H., Jr. & Stone, A. R. (1957). Why patients leave psychotherapy. *A.M.A. Archives of Neurology and Psychiatry, 77,* 284–299.

Fuchs, C. Z., & Rehm, L. P. (1977). A self-control behavior therapy program for depression. *Journal of Consulting and Clinical Psychology, 45,* 206–215.

Galassi, J. P., DeLo, J. S., Galassi, M. D., & Bastien, S. (1974). The College Self-Expression Scale: A measure of assertiveness. *Behavior Therapy, 5,* 165–171.

Galassi, M. D., & Galassi, J. P. (1977). *Assert yourself! How to be your own person.* New York: Human Sciences Press.

Gambrill, E. D., & Richey, C. A. (1975). An assertion inventory for use in assessment and research. *Behavior Therapy, 6,* 550—561.

Gansler, D., Heimberg, R. G., & Becker, R. E. (1985, November). *Analysis of Beck Depression Inventory and Hamilton Rating Scale for Depression scores for major depressive and dysthymic patients.* Paper presented at the 19th annual meeting of the Association for the Advancement of Behavior Therapy, Houston, TX.

Garber, J., & Seligman, M. E. P. (1980). *Human helplessness.* New York: Academic Press.

Gay, M. L., Hollandsworth, J. G., & Galassi, J. P. An assertiveness inventory for adults. *Journal of Counseling Psychology*, 1975, 22, 340—344.

Gibbon, M., McDonald-Scott, P., & Endicott, J. (1981). Mastering the art of research interviewing. *Archives of General Psychiatry*, 38, 1259-1262.

Gottman, J. M., Notarius, C., Markman, H., Bank, S., Yoppi, B., & Rubin, M. E. (1976). Behavior exchange theory and marital decision making. *Journal of Personality and Social Psychology*, 34, 14-23.

Gurtman, M. B. (1986). Depression and the response of others: Reevaluating the reevaluation. *Journal of Abnormal Psychology*, 95, 99-101.

Hamilton, M. (1960). A rating scale for depression. *Journal of Neurology, Neurosurgery, and Psychiatry*, 23, 56-62.

Hamilton, M. (1967). Development of a rating scale for primary depressive illness. *British Journal of Psychiatry*, 6, 278-296.

Hammen, C., & Peters, S. D. (1978). Interpersonal consequences of depression: Responses to men and women enacting a depressed role. *Journal of Abnormal Psychology*, 87, 322-332.

Hammen, C., Mayol, A., deMayo, R., & Marks, T. (1986). Initial symptom levels and the life-event-depression relationship. *Journal of Abnormal Psychology*, 95, 114-122.

Hedlund, J. L., & Vieweg, B. W. (1979). The Hamilton Rating Scale for Depression: A comprehensive review. *Journal of Operational Psychiatry*, 10, 149-165.

Hersen, M., Bellack, A. S., Himmelhoch, J. M., & Thase, M. E. (1984). Effects of social skills training, amitriptyline, and psychotherapy in unipolar depressed women. *Behavior Therapy*, 15, 21-40.

Hersen, M., Bellack, A. S., & Turner, S. M., Williams, M. T., Harper, K., & Watts, J. G. Psychometric properties of the Wolpe-Lazarus Assertiveness Scale. *Behaviour Research and Therapy*, 1979, 17, 63—69.

Hersen, M., Eisler, R., Miller, P. M. Johnson, M. B., & Pinkston, S. G. Effects of practice, instructions, and modeling on components of assertive behavior. *Behaviour Research and Therapy*, 1973, 11, 443-451.

Howes, M. J., & Hokanson, J. E. (1979). Conversational and social responses to depressive interpersonal behavior. *Journal of Abnormal Psychology*, 88, 625-634.

Jacobson, N. S., & Anderson, E. A. (1982). Interpersonal skill and depression in college students: An analysis of the timing of self-disclosures. *Behavior Therapy*, 13, 271-282.

Kanfer, F. H. (1970). Self-regulation: Research issues and speculations. In C. Neuinger & J. L. Michael (Eds.), *Behavior modification in clinical psychology*. New York: Appleton-Century-Crofts.

Kanfer, F. H. (1971). The maintenance of behavior by self-generated stimuli and reinforcement. In A. Jacobs & L. B. Sachs (Eds.), *The psychology of private events: Perspectives on covert response systems*. New York: Academic Press.

Kazdin, A. E. (1974). Reactive self-monitoring: The effects of response desirability, goal setting, and feedback. *Journal of Consulting and Clinical Psychology*, 42, 704-716.

Kelly, J. A., Kern, J. M., Kirkley, B. G., Patterson, J. N., & Keane, T. M. (1980). Reactions to assertive versus unassertive behavior: Differential effects for males and females and implications for assertiveness training. *Behavoir Therapy*, 11, 670-682.

King, D. A., & Heller, K. (1984). Depression and the response of others: A re-evaluation. *Journal of Abnormal Psychology*, 93, 477-480.

Klerman, G. L., & Weissman, M. M. (1982). Interpersonal psychotherapy: Theory and research. In A. J. Rush (Ed.), *Short term therapies for depression: Behavioral, interpersonal, cognitive and psychodynamic approaches* (pp. 88-104). New York: Guilford Press.

Kuiper, N. A., & McCabe, S. B. (1985). The appropriateness of social topics: Effects of depression and cognitive vulnerability on self and other judgments. *Cognitive Therapy and Research*, 9, 317-379.

Langone, M. (1979). Assertiveness and Lewinsohn's theory of depression: An empirical test. *The Behavior Therapist, 2,* 21.

Lea, G., & Pacquin, M. (1981). Assertiveness and clinical depression. *The Behavior Therapist, 4,* 9–10.

Lewinsohn, P. M. (1975). The behavioral study and treatment of depression. In M. Hersen, R. M. Eisler, & P. M. Miller (Eds.), *Progress in behavior modification: Vol. 1.* New York: Academic Press.

Lewinsohn, P. M., Mischel, W., Chaplin, W., & Barton, R. (1980). Social competence and depression: The role of illusory self-perceptions. *Journal of Abnormal Psychology, 89,* 203–212.

Lewinsohn, P. M., Youngren, M. A., & Grosscup, S. (1979). Depression and reinforcement. In R. A. DePue (Ed.), *The psychobiology of depressive disorders.* New York: Academic Press.

Libet, J., & Lewinsohn, P. M. (1973). The concept of social skill with special reference to the behavior of depressed persons. *Journal of Consulting and Clinical Psychology, 40,* 304–312.

Lubin, B. (1981). *Manual for the Depression Adjective Checklists.* San Diego: Educational and Industrial Testing Service.

Luborsky, L. (1962). Clinicians' judgements of mental health. *Archives of General Psychiatry, 7,* 407–417.

McFall, R. M., & Lillesand, D. B. (1971). Behavior rehearsal with modeling and coaching in assertion training. *Journal of Abnormal Psychology, 77,* 313–323.

Metcalfe, M., & Goldman, E. (1965). Validation of an inventory for measuring depression. *British Journal of Psychiatry, 111,* 240–242.

Meyers, J. K., Weissman, M. M., Tischler, G. L., Holzer, C. E. III, Leaf, P. J., Orvaschel, H., Anthony, J. C., Boyd, J. H., Burke, J. D., Jr., Kramer, M., & Stoltzman, R. (1984). Six-month prevalence of psychiatric disorders in three communities. *Archives of General Psychiatry, 41,* 959–967.

Morrison, R. L., & Bellack, A. S. (1981). The role of social perception in social skill. *Behavior Therapy, 12,* 69–80.

Nelson, R. O. (1977). Methodological issues in assessment via self-monitoring. In J. D. Cone & R. P. Hawkins (Eds.) *Behavioral assessment: New directions in clinical psychology* (pp. 217–240). New York: Brunner/Mazel.

O'Hara, M. W., & Rehm, L. P. (1983a), Hamilton Rating Scale for Depression: Reliability and validity of judgements of novice raters. *Journal of Consulting and Clinical Psychology, 51,* 318–319.

O'Hara, M. W., & Rehm, L. P. (1983b). Self-control group therapy of depression. In A. Freeman (Ed.), *Cognitive therapy with couples and groups* (pp. 67–94). New York: Plenum Press.

Parloff, M. B., Kelman, H. C., & Frank, J. D. (1954). Comfort, effectiveness, and self-awareness as criteria of improvement in psychotherapy. *American Journal of Psychiatry, 111,* 343–352.

Raskin, A., Schulterbrandt, J., Reatig, N., & McKeon, J. J. (1969). Replication of factors of psychopathology in interview, ward behavior, and self-report ratings of hospitalized depressives. *Journal of Nervous and Mental Disease, 148,* 87–98.

Raskin, A., Schulterbrandt, J., Reatig, N., & Rice, C. (1967). Factors of psychopathology in interview, ward behavior, and self-report ratings of hospitalized depressives. *Journal of Consulting Psychology, 31,* 270–278.

Rathus, S. A. A 30 item schedule for assessing assertive behavior. *Behavior Therapy, 1973, 4,* 398–406.

Rehm, L. P. (1977). A self-control model of depression. *Behavior Therapy, 8,* 787–804.

Rehm, L. P., Fuchs, C. Z., Roth, D. M., Kornblith, S. J., & Romano, J. M. (1979). A comparison of self-control and assertion skills, treatments of depression. *Behavior Therapy, 10,* 429–442.

Rehm, L. P., Kornblith, S. J., O'Hara, M. W., Lamparski, D. M., Romano, J. M., & Volkin, J. I. (1981). An evaluation of major components in a self-control therapy program for depression.

Behavior Modification, 5, 459–489.

Rimm, D. C., & Masters, J. C. (1974). *Behavior therapy: Techniques and empirical findings.* New York: Academic Press.

Robins, L. N., Helzer, J. E., Weissman, M. M., Orvaschel, H., Gruenberg, E., Burke, J. D., & Regier, D. A. (1984). Lifetime prevalence of specific psychiatric disorders in three sites. *Archives of General Psychiatry, 41*, 949–958.

Roth, D., Bielski, R., Jones, M., Parker, W., & Osborn, G. (1982). A comparison of self-control therapy and combined self-control therapy and antidepressant medication in the treatment of depression. *Behavior Therapy, 13*, 133–144.

Roth, D., Rehm, L. P., & Rozensky, R. A. (1975). *Depression and self-reinforcement.* Unpublished manuscript, University of Pittsburgh.

Rozensky, R. A., Rehm, L. P., Pry, G., & Roth, D. (1974). *Depression and self-reinforcement in hospital patients.* Unpublished manuscript, University of Pittsburgh.

Rush, A. J., & Beck, A. T. (1978). Adults with affective disorders. In M. Hersen & A. S. Bellack (Eds.), *Behavior therapy in a psychiatric setting* (pp. 286–330). Baltimore: Williams and Wilkins.

St. Lawrence, J. S., Hughes, E. F., Goff, A. F., & Palmer, M. B. (1983). Assessment of role-play generalization across qualitatively different situations. *Journal of Behavioral Assessment, 5*, 289–307.

Sanchez, V., & Lewinsohn, P. M. (1980). Assertive behavior and depression. *Journal of Consulting and Clinical Psychology, 48*, 119–120.

Schwab, J. J., Bell, R. A. Warheit, G. J., & Schwab, R. B. (1979). *Social order and mental health: The Florida health study.* New York: Brunner/Mazel.

Spitzer, R., Endicott, J., & Robins, E. (May, 1977). *Research diagnostic criteria: Rationale and review.* Paper presented at the meeting of the American Psychiatric Association, Toronto.

Spitzer, R., Endicott, J., & Robins, E. (1978). Research diagnostic criteria: Rationale and reliability. *Archives of General Psychiatry, 34*, 773–782.

Strack, S., & Coyne, J. C. (1983). Social confirmation of dysphora: Shared and private reactions to depression, *Journal of Personality and Social Psychology, 44*, 798–806.

Thase, M. E., Hersen, H., Bellack, A. S., Himmelhoch, J. M., & Kupfer, D. J. (1983). Validation of a Hamilton subscale for endogenomorphic depression. *Journal of Affective Disorders, 5*, 267–278.

Vincent, J. P., Friedman, L. L., Nugent, J., & Messerly, L. (1979). Demand characteristics in observations of marital interaction. *Journal of Consulting and Clinical Psychology, 47*, 557–566.

Weissman, M. M., & Meyers, J. K. (1978). Affective disorders in an urban community. *Archives of General Psychiatry, 35*, 1304–1311.

Weissman, M. M., Wickramarante, P., Merikaneas, K. R., Leckman, J. F., Prusoff, B. A., Caruso, K. A., Kidd, K. K., & Gammon, G. D. (1984). Onset of major depression in early adulthood. *Archives of General Psychiatry, 41*, 1136–1143.

Wener, A., & Rehm, L. P. (1975). Depressive affect: A test of behavioral hypotheses. *Journal of Abnormal Psychology, 84*, 221–227.

Whybrow, P. C., Akiskal, H. S., & McKinney, W. T. (1984). *Mood disorders: Toward a new psychobiology.* New York: Plenum.

Williams, J. G., Barlow, D. H., & Agras, W. S. (1972). Behavioral measurement of severe depression. *Archives of General Psychiatry, 27*, 330–333.

Wills, T. A., Weiss, R. L., & Patterson, G. R. (1974). A behavioral analysis of the determinants of marital satisfaction. *Journal of Consulting and Clinical Psychology, 42*, 802–811.

Wolpe, J., & Lazarus, A. A. (1966). *Behavior therapy techniques: A guide to the treatment of neuroses.* Oxford: Pergamon.

Youngren, M. A., & Lewinsohn, P. M. (1980). The functional relationship between depression and problematic interpersonal behavior. *Journal of Abnormal Psychology, 89,* 333–341.

Zung, W. W. K. (1967). Factors influencing the self-rating depression scale. *Archives of General Psychiatry, 16,* 543–547.

Zung, W. W. K. (1974). The measurement of affects: Depression and anxiety. In P. Pichot & R. Oliver-Martin (Eds.), *Psychological measurements in psychopharmacology.* Basel, Switzerland: S. Karger, AG.

Appendix
Role-Play Situations

Scene I.   My car is in the shop for repairs._____

                                                   (A female friend)
offers to give me a ride to and from work while my car is getting fixed. I am very pleased with her offer. She says

First
Prompt: I KNOW YOU WON'T HAVE YOUR CAR FOR A FEW DAYS. I'LL BE GLAD TO TAKE YOU TO WORK AND BRING YOU HOME IN THE EVENING.

Second
Prompt: I KNOW I HAD A PROBLEM GETTING AROUND THE LAST TIME MY CAR WAS IN THE GARAGE GETTING FIXED.

Scene II.   I've been working on a difficult job all week.

_____ comes over to me with a very pleased
      (A female supervisor)
smile on her face. She says

First
Prompt: THAT'S A VERY GOOD JOB YOU'VE DONE, I LIKE YOUR WORK.

Second
Prompt: I DON'T SAY THIS VERY OFTEN, BUT I WANTED YOU TO KNOW I APPRECIATE YOUR WORK.

Scene III.   I'm doing the laundry. _____ is working in
                                  (A female relative)
the yard. The phone begins to ring. She yells from the garage

First
Prompt: I'LL GET IT FOR YOU.

Second
Prompt: WHEN YOU FINISH THE LAUNDRY, I'LL HELP YOU FOLD THE CLOTHES.

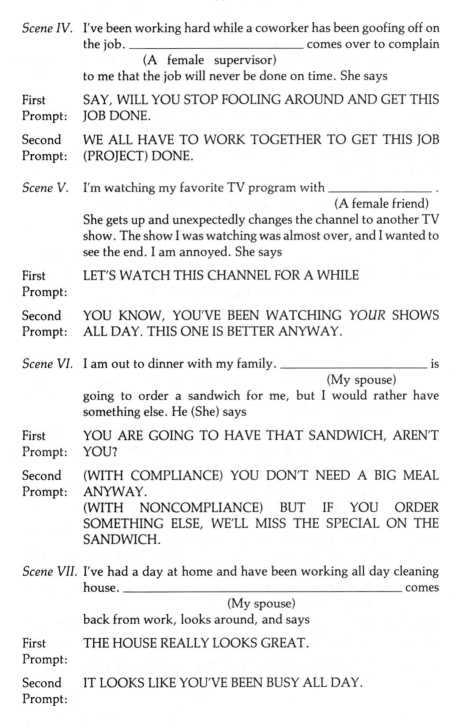

Scene IV. I've been working hard while a coworker has been goofing off on the job. _____ comes over to complain
(A female supervisor)
to me that the job will never be done on time. She says

First   SAY, WILL YOU STOP FOOLING AROUND AND GET THIS
Prompt: JOB DONE.

Second   WE ALL HAVE TO WORK TOGETHER TO GET THIS JOB
Prompt: (PROJECT) DONE.

Scene V. I'm watching my favorite TV program with _____ .
(A female friend)
She gets up and unexpectedly changes the channel to another TV show. The show I was watching was almost over, and I wanted to see the end. I am annoyed. She says

First   LET'S WATCH THIS CHANNEL FOR A WHILE
Prompt:

Second   YOU KNOW, YOU'VE BEEN WATCHING *YOUR* SHOWS
Prompt: ALL DAY. THIS ONE IS BETTER ANYWAY.

Scene VI. I am out to dinner with my family. _____ is
(My spouse)
going to order a sandwich for me, but I would rather have something else. He (She) says

First   YOU ARE GOING TO HAVE THAT SANDWICH, AREN'T
Prompt: YOU?

Second   (WITH COMPLIANCE) YOU DON'T NEED A BIG MEAL
Prompt: ANYWAY.
(WITH NONCOMPLIANCE) BUT IF YOU ORDER SOMETHING ELSE, WE'LL MISS THE SPECIAL ON THE SANDWICH.

Scene VII. I've had a day at home and have been working all day cleaning house. _____ comes
(My spouse)
back from work, looks around, and says

First   THE HOUSE REALLY LOOKS GREAT.
Prompt:

Second   IT LOOKS LIKE YOU'VE BEEN BUSY ALL DAY.
Prompt:

*Scene VIII.*_____ comes to town to visit me.
              (A good male friend)
              I really wanted to keep in touch with him and have been writing to
              him for the past year. As the two of us are driving home from the
              terminal, he says

First   I REALLY ENJOYED YOUR LETTERS. YOU'RE THE ONLY
Prompt: FRIEND I CAN COUNT ON TO STAY IN TOUCH.

Second   IT'S HARD TO KEEP IN TOUCH WHEN WE LIVE SO FAR
Prompt: APART.

Scene IX. It's an hour before quitting time and _____
                                        (A male supervisor)
             has some mail to be dropped off at the post office. He says

First   I KNOW THAT THE POST OFFICE IS ON YOUR WAY
Prompt: HOME. WOULD YOU PLEASE DROP THESE OFF THERE,
            AND YOU CAN LEAVE FROM THERE.

Second   I NOTICED YOU WERE WORKING HARD TODAY, AND
Prompt: YOU DESERVE TO LEAVE EARLY.

Scene X.   I've been home all day watching TV. I haven't been feeling well
             and haven't been able to sign some papers. _____
                                        (My male relative)
             comes in and says

First   YOU'VE BEEN WATCHING TV ALL DAY. I SUPPOSE YOU
Prompt: HAVEN'T SIGNED THOSE INSURANCE PAPERS I GAVE
            YOU YESTERDAY?

Second   YOU KNEW I'D BE COMING HERE AT THIS TIME. WHY
Prompt: DON'T YOU GET UP AND LOOK AT THEM NOW?

Scene XI. I had a very busy day at work and am tired.
             _____ comes in and asks me to stay late for the
                 (Male supervisor)
             third time this week. I really feel that I would like to go home
             tonight. He says

First   I'M LEAVING NOW. WOULD YOU MIND STAYING LATE
Prompt: AGAIN AND FINISHING THIS WORK FOR ME?

Second   THERE'S A DEADLINE FOR THIS JOB, AND WE NEED TO
Prompt: GET IT DONE.

Scene XII. _____ asks me to join him and some
(A male friend)
other friends in the country. I tell him I don't feel like going today.
He says

First   I THINK YOU STAY IN THE HOUSE TOO MUCH. WHY
Prompt: DON'T YOU COME ALONG?

Second   WE WERE COUNTING ON YOU COMING ALONG. WE
Prompt: WON'T TAKE NO FOR AN ANSWER.

Author Index

103

Subject Index

About the Authors

Robert E. Becker, Ph.D., State University of New York at Albany (1977) is Associate Professor of Psychiatry at the Medical College of Pennsylvania and Director of the Psychology Internship Training Program. He is author or co-author of many journal articles and book chapters, including several about social skills training and its use as a treatment for depresssion. Professor Becker has been a principal or co-principal investigator on several National Institute of Mental Health grants concerned with the assessment or treatment of depression and anxiety disorders. He recently received a diplomate in clinical psychology from the American Board of Professional Psychology.

Richard G. Heimberg, Ph.D., Florida State University (1977) is Associate Professor of Psychology at the State University of New York at Albany and Research Associate at the University's Center for Stress and Anxiety Disorders, where he directs the treatment program for individuals with social fears and phobias. He has published over 40 articles on the topics of depression, social skills training, and cognitive-behavior therapy.

Alan S. Bellack, Ph.D., Pennsylvania State University (1970) is Professor of Psychiatry at the Medical College of Pennsylvania and Adjunct Professor of Psychology at Temple University. He was formerly Professor of Psychology and Psychiatry and Director of Clinical Psychology Training at the University of Pittsburgh. He is Past-President of the Association for Advancement of Behavior Therapy, and a Fellow of Division 12 of APA. Professor Bellack is co-author and co-editor of 18 books including: *The Clinical Psychology Handbook, International Handbook of Behavior Modification and Therapy, Behavioral Assessment: A Practical Handbook, Third Edition.* He has published over 90 journal articles and has received numerous National Institute of Mental Health research grants on social skills, behavioral assessment, and schizophrenia, and with Michel Hersen he is co-editor and co-founder of the journals *Behavior Modification* and *Clinical Psychology Review*. He has served on the editorial boards of numerous journals and has been consultant to a number of publishing companies and mental health facilities as well as the National Institute of Mental Health.

Psychology Practitioner Guidebooks

Editors
Arnold P. Goldstein, Syracuse University
Leonard Krasner, Stanford University & SUNY at Stony Brook
Sol L. Garfield, Washington University

Elsie M. Pinkston & Nathan L. Linsk – CARE OF THE ELDERLY: A Family Approach

Donald Meichenbaum – STRESS INOCULATION TRAINING
Sebastiano Santostefano – COGNITIVE CONTROL THERAPY WITH CHILDREN AND ADOLESCENTS

Lillie Weiss, Melanie Katzman & Sharlene Wolchik – TREATING BULIMIA: A Psychoeducational Approach

Edward B. Blanchard & Frank Andrasik – MANAGEMENT OF CHRONIC HEADACHES: A Psychological Approach

Raymond G. Romanczyk – CLINICAL UTILIZATION OF MICROCOMPUTER TECHNOLOGY

Philip H. Bornstein & Marcy T. Bornstein – MARITAL THERAPY: A Behavioral-Communications Approach

Michael T. Nietzel & Ronald C. Dillehay – PSYCHOLOGICAL CONSULTATION IN THE COURTROOM

Elizabeth B. Yost, Larry E. Beutler, M. Anne Corbishley & James R. Allender – GROUP COGNITIVE THERAPY: A Treatment Method for Depressed Older Adults

Lillie Weiss – DREAM ANALYSIS IN PSYCHOTHERAPY

Edward A. Kirby & Liam K. Grimley – UNDERSTANDING AND TREATING ATTENTION DEFICIT DISORDER

Jon Eisenson – LANGUAGE AND SPEECH DISORDERS IN CHILDREN

Eva L. Feindler & Randolph B. Ecton– ADOLESCENT ANGER CONTROL: Cognitive-Behavioral Techniques

Michael C. Roberts – PEDIATRIC PSYCHOLOGY: Psychological Interventions and Strategies for Pediatric Problems

Daniel S. Kirschenbaum, William G. Johnson & Peter M. Stalonas, Jr. – TREATING CHILDHOOD AND ADOLESCENT OBESITY

W. Stewart Agras – EATING DISORDERS: Management of Obesity, Bulimia and Anorexia Nervosa

Ian H. Gotlib & Catherine A. Colby – TREATMENT OF DEPRESSION: An Interpersonal Systems Approach

Walter B. Pryzwansky & Robert N. Wendt – PSYCHOLOGY AS A PROFESSION: Foundations of Practice

Cynthia D. Belar, William W. Deardorff & Karen E. Kelly – THE PRACTICE OF CLINICAL HEALTH PSYCHOLOGY

Paul Karoly & Mark P. Jensen – MULTIMETHOD ASSESSMENT OF CHRONIC PAIN

William L. Golden, E. Thomas Dowd & Fred Friedberg – HYPNOTHERAPY: A Modern Approach

Patricia Lacks – BEHAVIORAL TREATMENT FOR PERSISTENT INSOMNIA

Arnold P. Goldstein & Harold Keller – AGGRESSIVE BEHAVIOR: Assessment and Intervention

C. Eugene Walker, Barbara L. Bonner & Keith L. Kaufman – THE PHYSICALLY AND SEXUALLY ABUSED CHILD: Evaluation and Treatment

Robert E. Becker, Richard G. Heimberg & Alan S. Bellack – SOCIAL SKILLS TRAINING TREATMENT FOR DEPRESSION

Richard F. Dangel & Richard A. Polster – TEACHING CHILD MANAGEMENT SKILLS